NATURE,
CHILDREN
and YOU

NATURE, CHILDREN and YOU

Revised edition

By Paul E. Goff

OHIO UNIVERSITY PRESS
Athens, Ohio • London

Library of Congress Cataloging in Publication Data

Goff, Paul E.
  Nature, children, and you

  1. Natural history—Study and teaching.
2. Natural history—Outdoor books. I. Title.
QH51.G57   1982   372.3'57   81-18911
ISBN 0-8214-0607-8   AACR2
ISBN 0-8214-0679-5 (pbk.)

To my daughter, Michelle Suzanne, who reconfirmed my faith in the spiritual values of nature which flow through sensitive children to understanding adults.

CONTENTS

Introduction

Urbanization prevents most of us from growing our own foods, pumping our own water, and performing other essential, close-to-nature functions of life. Through technology we keep ourselves supplied with eggs, meat, dairy products, and other physical necessities—grown, managed, or produced by the few who remain in rural areas. But statistics reveal something vital is missing from our lives even though we seem to have plenty of life-sustaining items.

People are rapidly losing emotional stability along with those spiritual and cultural values which result from a kinship with the natural world. Too many people are not content, have not "found themselves" or do not feel their lives are meaningful. We have become so dependent upon machines that we have lost much of our self-reliance. We have forgotten that it is possible to travel three blocks down the street without an automobile. Technology has not found a way to package, freeze, and transport those feelings which are acquired only among natural surroundings. Unlike eggs, meat, and other food items, such feelings have not followed man into his urban developments. But man must learn how to acquire such feelings in spite of certain unchangeable circumstances.

I marvel at modern man's achievements. The fact that fresh lobsters can be flown daily into our most inland cities and served with a large assortment of foods from all over the world is remarkable. It also is regrettable that many persons cannot partake of these foods because of ulcers, nervous stomachs, and other disorders resulting primarily from the tensions within the urban developments which they have helped to create.

The telephone is a working miracle—we have the best means of communication the world has ever known. Yet, when problems occur in various businesses and organizations, they are called "communications problems." People find it easier to talk to someone they do not know in some distant city than to communicate with their neighbors, spouses, or children.

The purpose of this book is not to point out the hopelessness of various situations, all the perplexing environmental problems, or controversial issues concerning moral and social decay. Neither is it designed merely to catalogue and categorize numerous facts, factors, and theories. Like many others, I am well aware of pessimistic situations and often have been labelled a pessimist. But I am also aware of a ray of hope that can become reality if enough people will turn toward it. I believe most of our major problems are merely symptoms resulting from a lack of proper mental or emotional nourishment. People will have to retrace their footsteps to the world of nature in order to acquire certain mental vitamins. This does not mean a mass migration back to country living—I am not suggesting what most people would consider an impossibility. This book is designed to help people derive the most meaningful, exclusive benefits from any natural area they may be in. And this can be a vacant city lot, a farmer's woodlot, or a huge national park. It can be any situation in which natural phenomena or natural processes occur.

We are emphasizing the fact that many meanings, concepts, and principles can be derived from nature. These pages are simply the sharing of one person's experiences with nature and people. They are written by one who has lived in rural as well as city situations and who has made a career out of helping others secure more enjoyment and meaning from nature through an increased awareness and understanding of its many wonders.

The information can be as meaningful to one who cannot tell the difference between an oak and a maple as it is to one who is an expert at identification.

When a person has grown up in a rural setting, moved to a city environment, and then worked with city people who visit natural areas, he becomes aware of many significant facts. For twenty-two years I have been leading groups on nature walks which have been called "interpretive walks," "discovery hikes," "sensitivity walks," and various other names. But all of them amounted to the same thing—sharing feelings for, as well as information about, various natural phenomena. And I have become aware of the fact that most children and adults prefer a simple approach. They like to participate by asking questions and relating some of their own experiences; they like to hear new ways of expressing feelings for common forms of life. They prefer to discover on their own, and they like to be complimented for using their senses. Through experiences with parents, teachers, leaders, and children, I firmly believe that any adult or any youngster with a mature attitude has the capability of playing the role of an interpretive naturalist.

Children should be able to look to their parents, teachers, Scout leaders, camp counselors, and other group leaders as sources of nature understanding and enjoyment. When children return home from a camp experience or nature walk, they should be able to have a two-way conversation with their parents.

Often a child goes home from a meaningful outdoor experience and begins talking to his mother, who has been busy with housework, or with his father, who has been in an office, factory, or other indoor situation. The enthusiastic youngster sometimes experiences a great disappointment.

Before children can expound on their new experiences in the out-of-doors, one or the other of their parents will say, "All right, you had a real good time but it's over now—maybe you can go again sometime." Or, they might grumble, "We've got more to worry about than butterflies and flowers—they're not going to pay the bills around here."

What a difference it would make if parents could become involved in the conversations which their children try to begin.

A child's eyes would really light up if his parents would tell him something new and meaningful about a natural phenomenon he had seen or sensed.

For example, suppose a little girl came home from day camp or a school nature walk and said, "We saw a whole field full of daisies." Then, suppose her father would ask, "Do you know how the daisy got its name?"

The father would proceed to ask his daughter what part of the human face this round flower cluster resembles. She would reply, "The eye." Her dad could then say, "That's right, and were the daisies blooming during the daytime or at night?" His daughter might say, "Well, it was daytime when I saw them."

Finally, the father would explain that the round flower cluster once was called "the eye of the day" or the "day's eye." Hence, the name, "daisy."

Did you know how the daisy's name was derived? There are many who have never given this any thought. If you have any doubt, ask the next dozen people you meet if they know how the daisy got its name. For many reasons, people are not aware of interesting facts related to common forms of life with which they are well acquainted.

When you explain the significance of the name of the daisy, you are playing the role of an interpretive naturalist. You are making a natural phenomenon more meaningful to others. When daisies are seen again, they'll be enjoyed and appreciated more.

If you think this type of approach is more valuable than giving the scientific name of the daisy, this is your type of book. This is what we're trying to share—meaningful bits of information, concepts of nature appreciation, and techniques of interpreting natural phenomena for others.

You may wonder why so much emphasis is being placed upon nature as it relates to children or you may be saying, "Aren't adults important, too?" To prevent adults from feeling neglected, we must accept certain basic understandings.

We are concerned with unique, enjoyable experiences attainable in the out-of-doors. In order to take full advantage of many rewarding opportunities, we require three essentials—nature, children, and you.

Instead of regarding this text as a means by which adults can help children, consider it a means by which adults can utilize children and nature to enrich their own lives. All three will benefit—adults' lives will become more meaningful and enjoyable; children's lives will be filled with new hopes, thrills, and wonders; and nature, itself, will have a more secure future. Adults and children create a two-way street through the fields and woodlands. A scientist might label this a "symbiotic relationship" with nature playing the role of a catalytic agent. But someone has to take the initiative.

The responsibilities of planning, organizing, and initiating nature activities should rest upon the shoulders of adults. It seems more sensible to tell adults how to utilize children and nature than to tell children how they might utilize adults and nature.

One could ask, "Why not tell adults how to work with other adults in the out-of-doors?" This would be a fair question and could be answered in several ways.

Adults, generally, are not so receptive to ideas and suggestions pertaining to natural concepts. All of us have been caught up in the world of artificiality; with added responsibilities of adulthood, we are forced to look at things in a monetary manner. By looking at nature through the eyes of children we once again can be reminded of the wonders, pertaining to natural phenomena, which we have come to regard as commonplace. Children have a way of looking at things for what they are.

For example, if I placed a dollar bill and a shiny new dime on a table in front of a two-year-old child, the child might reach for the dime instead of the dollar. The dime might seem more attractive or the child might be fascinated by the way it can spin and make noise on a flat surface. The child's reaction involves nothing but the use of the senses. This is why a youngster might be more interested in a caterpillar or earthworm than in some rare warbler that thrills a seasoned, adult, bird enthusiast. This is also why experts at identification are not necessarily the best nature leaders.

Most techniques which work with children will work with adults if one adjusts his vocabulary. And, in a sense, anyone being introduced to nature for the first time is a child to nature, regardless of his age.

Another reason for the emphasis on children results from my

working with thousands of children and observing a steady, alarming trend away from basic understandings about the natural environments which are close to them. Nature is close to most of our cities, but too many kids remain trapped within an urban setting. Today's children are farther removed from nature than were children of preceding generations; that is, the parents and the grandparents of most children have been reared in urban surroundings. This background probably accounts for youngsters' asking if there are monkeys in the woods, crocodiles in the ponds, or elephants out in the grassy fields. The only introduction they have had to nature has been through movies and television shows where the main nature topics have centered around jungle safaris and sensational natural phenomena of faraway lands. Yet I have observed and know from experience that these same children, when provided opportunities, become more excited over common forms of life in their own regions.

Nature is about the only thing left where principles and laws hold true; where things are as they are supposed to be; where there is no discrimination against anyone; and where beauty, harmony, and interrelatedness provide experiences that people enjoy remembering. One is never too young or too old to become involved in learning about nature.

How and Why
I Became a Naturalist

The value of nature to children seems important to me because of my background which included living in a rural area until I was eight. While not all my childhood companions became naturalists, I have, from time to time, met and talked with some of them. Any mention of outdoor experiences we shared as children makes their eyes light up and they readily admit some of these experiences are their most cherished memories. They retain feelings of gratitude and respect for those adults who made it possible for us to enjoy various outdoor adventures.

I was born in the hills of eastern Ohio, near the village of Colerain in Belmont County. I can remember back to the age of three or four, and my most vivid memory concerns the night when a skunk was after the chickens in my parents' chicken coop.

A strange odor drifted through our house and all the chickens were squawking. My parents, older brother, and sisters ran out of the house all alarmed about the "polecat" that was after the chickens. I envisioned the polecat as an elephant-sized cat that carried a large pole for clubbing chickens and people. The chicken coop was hidden from view, and I was frightened as the others disappeared into the darkness of the path leading to the chicken coop.

As I peered out over the back porch, I noticed a large white clump on the floor and thought it was something deposited by the polecat—the source of the strange odor that filled the air. Later, the others returned to the house; the polecat had run away, and the next morning I discovered that the while clump on the porch floor was nothing but a white towel. I also learned that a neighbor's dog had caused the skunk to release its spray.

After days of playing in the fields and woodlands near our house, we often sat on a glider on the front porch. The summer air became more moist and cool in the evenings and was saturated with various fragrances—honeysuckle, roses, and black locust blossoms. Frequently, we detected the odor of a "polecat" or skunk. I cannot remember when it was, but I finally learned that "polecat" is simply another name for the common skunk.

Today, friends think I'm somewhat odd when I tell them how much I enjoy the aroma of a skunk. Often, while driving along country roads, we detect a faint odor of skunk. I immediately roll down the windows and open all the vents so as to let in the full blast of the aroma. As I take several deep breaths of the air and express my delight, my friends just shake their heads. What they do not realize is the fact that it is not so much the aroma that I enjoy, as all the pleasant memories of country living which the aroma recalls. There are at least a hundred other fragrances that would recall all kinds of memories and mysteries of rural life.

In the fall, I usually joined some of the older boys who gathered the fruits of the osage orange or hedge-apple. They called them "monkey balls." And acting like a bunch of monkeys, they threw them at one another along the highway in front of our house.

The "baseball" games with the osage oranges usually became battles, with participants seeing who could hit whom. I joined in the battles the best I could—about all I accomplished was getting sticky osage orange juice all over my hands and clothes. These fruits had a pleasant aroma, and when I get a chance to smell it today, I am taken back to that that little country home and highway covered with smashed "monkey balls."

In case you are wondering about the term "monkey ball," I would like to point out that no one had given us the book name for this particular tree. I guess the older boys came up with a name that was meaningful to them. "Osage orange" would not have meant much to any of us at that time.

During the latter part of the summer all of us children gathered the shed outer shells of the annual cicadas or locusts. I would usually have a dozen or so of these to play with—they were cows, dogs, cats, or anything else I wanted them to be. Once I had a live cicada which had not yet shed its skin, and it was better than a wind-up toy, being able to move around all by itself.

I still remember those cold autumn evenings when my parents and several relatives would make black walnut taffy. Some would crack the walnuts and pick out the meat while the others prepared to cook the candy. They would pour the mixture, when it reached the right temperature, onto a large slab. Walnuts were added to the taffy before two people with butter rubbed all over their hands began pulling and twisting the taffy back and forth between them.

After pulling the taffy until it reached the right consistency, which they could tell from experience, one or the other would say, "It's ready." Long strands of the soft candy were laid out on the buttered slab and creased with a knife. After the candy had cooled and hardened, it was broken along the creases and the chunks were stacked in bowls and plates. These memories cross my mind whenever I taste black walnut candy of any kind.

I had other experiences which had little or nothing to do with nature except for the fact that they occurred at a time in my life when I was communing with nature on a daily basis. Therefore, certain non-natural phenomena bring back pleasant memories. The whine of truck tires on a highway on a quiet summer day and their gradual fading away, an old threshing machine next to a road, book satchels, crayons, and talk of school—these bring back memories of screech owls calling in the night, calls of cicadas and katydids, pretty autumn leaves, and the first fall of snow.

When I was four, my parents decided to move to another house about three miles away. The front of our new house faced a concrete highway, less traveled than the former one. In the front lawn were two large white pines. Between the pines ran a flag-stone walk, ending near the highway between two faded greenish gray posts. In summer these posts were covered with a beautiful climbing rose. The new home had two stories plus a cellar. It also had a large front porch covered by a roof supported by large, round white pillars.

At one end of our porch were a flagstone patio and the pump. Behind the pump, in a shaded area, was a large bed of lilies of the valley. Our house and the highway which ran in front of it were on the side of a hill. This hill continued to slope away from the back of our house to a little creek; a pathway led from the porch down the hill and then forked, with one fork going to the outhouse and the other going down the hill to a fence. This was a barbed wire fence with a split rail section in the middle; this is where the path met the fence and the point where we usually went over or through it. Being the smallest in our family, I could easily scoot on my belly under the lowest strand of barbed wire.

Why am I telling you about these experiences when I know they cannot possibly have the same significance for anyone else that they have for me? Before going any further, I want you to know that many of those experiences will be referred to in other parts of this book. They will be used in making analogies and comparisons; they provide a base for many broad concepts and they will, I hope, prove why certain techniques, procedures, and attitudes are successful when one is interpreting nature for others. The experiences I enjoyed in a rural atmosphere had as great a value as those offered by many colleges and universities. If you read these pages carefully, you will readily understand why I sometimes tell people that I went to college before entering the first grade—I tell them it was "Dr. Greenfield's College."

My father always had flower gardens and vegetable gardens. In addition, he had a large apple orchard. Those were depression days and many people grew and processed their own foods. I remember my parents making apple butter or chili sauce in a large kettle over an open fire. The shelves in our cellar were lined with jars of canned fruits and vegetables. The cellar also contained an apple bin and a potato bin. My dad could never leave the potato patch alone; in late summer, about every three days, he would dig down into the ground around a potato plant to see how the potatoes were developing. If he found a good-sized potato, he would break it loose from the root, cover the rest of the smaller potatoes and bring the large one into the house. Finally, the time would arrive to dig up all the potatoes.

Digging potatoes seemed like an exciting treasure hunt. As we went from clump to clump, we wondered how many potatoes would be under the ground and how large they might be. Sometimes we found some that were four or five inches in diameter.

I still remember one that must have been eight inches long and five inches wide—it was a real prize. This is where I learned one of my first important lessons.

When the large potato was peeled and cut across, we discovered it was hollow. I am not certain but I think this is where I first heard my parents use the expression, "Don't judge a book by its cover," or "All that glitters is not gold."

We also grew our own asparagus, rhubarb, and horseradish. In the spring it seemed as though we had asparagus and rhubarb for every other meal—I can remember eating cooked rhubarb for breakfast. And there was plenty of rhubarb pie around the house during the spring. Some of us liked to eat the rhubarb stalks raw; we would hold the pink stalk in one hand and keep dabbing it into sugar in our other hand. As we chewed the rhubarb, the sweetness would go away; but before it became too sour, we would mix it with the sugar. It was quite an art, maintaining the proper balance between the sweet sugar and the sour rhubarb. Our hands became quite a mess as did our clothes, but we had a good time.

My mother often made creamed asparagus which we ate with biscuits or bread. The most fascinating aspect of asparagus, however, was watching my father cut the fresh spears as they grew up out of the ground. In late summer, the asparagus that remained became small shrubs about five feet tall with delicate foliage and little red fruits. These plants resembled miniature Christmas trees decorated with tiny red ornaments.

Many of my dad's apples were made into cider; I remember a large barrel of cider in our cellar and how it turned to vinegar. I think a passerby, today, would be startled to hear someone shout, "Chase the mother away! You've got to chase the mother away!" But this is what one would have heard if he had passed our house at certain times.

The "mother" was mother of vinegar—that scum or slime

which forms when cider or wines are fermenting. We had to use a hose in order to siphon the vinegar out of the large barrel. The vinegar would begin to run out through the hose into a large jug, but before the jug was full, the mother would clog up the hose. When my brother, who usually did the siphoning, called upstairs and said all the vinegar was gone, he was told to chase the mother away. This was accomplished by blowing through the hose. I had my turn at this on at least one occasion. I didn't get my mouth off the hose in time, however, and got a mouth full of vinegar that gagged the living daylights out of me. That was real, unpasteurized, undiluted vinegar!

Once my dad gave me a load of parsnips which he placed in my small red wagon and told me to take them down the road and give them to a Mr. Best. This neighbor was delighted to receive so many parsnips, but I was puzzled by his remarks. He told me to tell my dad that he said, "Much obliged." The folks explained that this term meant "Thank you."

Mr. Best lived by a field which had been burned off one spring in preparation for plowing. I walked through it, sniffing the strange aroma of burnt grass. I found a small owl with its feathers charred, but didn't know whether it had really died in the fire. I always think of an owl when I smell burned grass.

Once we had a small live screech owl. We kept it under a lilac bush and nursed it back to health. My sisters named it "Nappy" because of its habit of blinking its eyes and looking so sleepy. We were saddened to see the owl fly away, never to return. As you have probably guessed, the aroma of lilac blossoms also makes me think of an owl.

It seemed we were always nibbling on something growing in the woods or fields or around the house. Sourgrass or wood sorrel, cheese mallow or what we called "button weed," grass stems, ripe elderberries, wild onions, nasturtium leaves, and many other plants or their fruits were eaten through the seasons. In spring, my dad would gather dandelions, dock, pokeweed sprouts, and other green plants, all of which he called "greens," and my mother would cook these with bacon strips. A little vinegar was added when we ate them. I was never too fond of greens, and I had the same attitude towards spinach.

In winter we made snow ice cream. On a cold day, we would

take bowls outdoors and scoop up some clean white snow. Over the snow we poured cream, sugar and a little vanilla extract. We remained outdoors and rapidly stirred this concoction. When all the ingredients were well blended, we thought we had ice cream. It didn't taste like regular ice cream but it did seem good enough to eat and we enjoyed making it.

My dad had a car, but I don't remember what it looked like. I do remember, however, that it was always a thrill to go for a ride. We visited many relatives living around the Ohio Valley, but the one I most enjoyed visiting was my Uncle Tom, who had a large farm.

My uncle was a full-time farmer whereas my father worked in a steel mill and on the WPA during the depression years. My uncle raised truck crops and animals; it seemed as though he had everything on that farm. Animals included cows, hogs, goats, work horses, chickens, turkeys, geese, and ducks. Truck crops and grains included cabbage, peppers, carrots, radishes, tomatoes, potatoes, several types of melons, cucumbers, corn, wheat, and oats.

The road back to my uncle's farm was full of bumps and ruts; it seemed as though it took forever to get there as we bounced around in the car. This farmhouse was very old. Betty Zane, who is well known in the history of the Ohio Valley, supposedly had spent several nights in this house long before my uncle lived there. Skunks lived under the house and their odor sometimes was quite prevalent when one of the dogs happened to disturb them.

The farm atmosphere was diffferent from that of our own home. Running a large farm was a lot of hard work, but my uncle and aunt plus their son and daughter managed to keep it going. They did their own butchering and made pounds of sausage and special types of lunch meats. They also had their own smokehouse where hams, bacon, and other meats were preserved with hickory smoke. There was a strange-looking device called a cream separator that sat in a cool, damp room just outside the kitchen. It was in this room that butter was churned and cottage cheese was made. We always referred to cottage cheese as "smear cheese."

I enjoyed making the rounds with my cousin as he fed the

chickens, gathered fresh eggs, milked the cows, and fed all the other animals. The hogs sometimes ate chunks of coal; chills ran up and down my spine as they crunched the coal between their teeth. But the most amusing sight was my cousin's squirting a stream of milk from the cow into the mouth of a cat standing on its back legs about three or four feet away.

Beyond the cultivated fields was a large wooded hill. We had many experiences in this woods, but the most memorable was the gathering of pawpaws in the fall. The pawpaw trees were located by looking for pawpaws that had already dropped to the ground; sometimes we could smell them in the air before spotting them. Once we found them, we looked up into the trees, which were seldom very large, and spotted pawpaws that hadn't fallen. Then we would shake the trees and scamper around gathering up the fresh pawpaws as they hit the ground. We couldn't eat many pawpaws at one time, for they were rich and filling.

In the evenings we sat on my uncle's large porch and watched the mist come in over the lowlands. This was the time of day for relaxation and talking. Some of us sat in chairs while others sat in swings. Once we saw a mother skunk and her young go waddling through the yard and down across a green meadow. It was fun staying overnight in the old farmhouse; in summer there was always a breeze coming through the windows in the upstairs bedroom. Watching the silky curtains drift back and forth from the open windows seemed to have a hypnotic effect. And early in the morning we were awakened by the crowing of many roosters—quite a contrast to the roar of city traffic which wakes me these days.

My uncle had several large blacksnakes living in his barn and would protect them from any visitor who tried to harm them. He said they were the best mouse and rat catchers on his farm. If he discovered a bird's nest on the ground when he was plowing, he would plow around it so the young could mature. When he planted corn, he would scatter several bushels at the edge of his cornfield for the crows. This kept the crows happy and prevented them from pulling up the planted corn. Uncle Tom had two large draft horses which were too old for work, but he had a love for them and could not send them off to a glue or fertilizer factory; he kept them until they died and then buried them on the farm. He sometimes took a special liking to a particular hog or steer and would not butcher it or send it off to market. He would keep it until it died of old age. Perhaps this was being overly sentimental, but I think kids, today, could benefit from being exposed to a few sentimental people to help balance their exposure to so many who have no love or reverence for anything except money and power.

Perhaps the greatest attraction for my brother, my four sisters, and me was the creek at the bottom of the hill behind our house. We had a large plank across it and here we would sit in the spring and summer with our bare feet in the water. It was fun making little fans in the current by letting our toes merely touch the water. It seemed as though we sat there for hours, letting the water tickle our toes. We often pushed our feet back into the current and then relaxed our leg muscles and allowed the current to push our feet forward again. When there was not enough current to make our little fans, we corrected the situation by swiftly pulling our toes through the water.

Upstream at the base of a large, rocky ledge was a quiet, clear pool. As we walked along the bank across from the ledge, we often saw frogs jump into the water. This also was a good place to see water snakes and "snake-feeders." The "snake-feeders" were actually dragonflies; some of the folks called them "snake-doctors." These harmless and beneficial insects supposedly fed and took care of sick snakes!

Perhaps the most fascinating feature of the creek was a large boulder which we called "the big rock." My brother, sisters, and I often went down to the big rock for our picnics. We sat on the boulder, eating tomato sandwiches and drinking lemonade. It was always quiet there except for the gurgling of water under and around the giant boulder. We often waded around in the water near the boulder or tried to cross the creek on smaller stepping stones. Every trip to the big rock was a new adventure.

While sitting on the boulder we saw schools of minnows, crawdads, frogs, and many other forms of aquatic life. We did not know the names of most small creatures, but we enjoyed watching them. Sometimes, we were lucky enough to see the kingfisher and green heron flying along the creek. While we were gazing into the clear water, a daydream often was interrupted by the shadow or reflection of one of these birds overhead.

Near the creek I learned to recognize the bloodroot, sweet William or phlox, violets, buttercups, and other common wild-flowers. My father once showed me the bright crimson sap in part of the bloodroot's rootstock. And I learned to enjoy the cinnamon odor of the sweet William blossoms.

The little creek was lined with patches of wild spearmint. As we walked along its banks and tramped through these patches, the aroma of spearmint filled the air. We often made spearmint tea from the dried leaves of this plant. To this day the taste or smell of spearmint brings back memories of a creek, a big rock, and numerous fascinating adventures.

Finally I reached the age of six; summer was giving way to autumn and there was talk of school. Tablets, book satchels, crayons, pencils, and other school supplies began to appear around the house. The calls of cicadas, katydids, crickets, and other fall insects signaled the beginning of a period of conflicts which has never ended.

Entering the first grade was a complete change in my daily routine; I couldn't walk down to the little stream, catch frogs, or see what was going on around the house. I didn't like the regimentation of the school room, and the only thing that helped overcome feelings of imprisonment was my having a teacher who taught what she called "science" in that first grade class. This science involved going outdoors whenever the weather was favorable—we looked at pretty leaves in the fall, animal tracks in the winter snow, and wildflowers in the spring. The teacher permitted us to see those things outdoors which we could never have seen indoors.

During the summer which followed, our family moved to northeastern Ohio into an industrial area where my father had found a better job. We lived about three miles north of the community of Sebring, located near the center of the Akron-Canton-Youngstown triangle. My parents rented a large house situated on a farm; our house was located between the farmer's house and his large barn. My brother and I spent a great deal of time with the farmer's son, who had just completed high school and had accepted much of the responsibility of running a large farm.

Each day on the farm was a new adventure, enhanced by the enthusiasm and understanding of the farmer's son, Jimmy.

The primary product of this farm was milk obtained from a large herd of Holstein cattle. Jimmy often took my brother and me along to the dairy where he delivered the milk in large milk cans. There we usually were treated to large ice cream cones which we ate on our way back to the farm. During the summer we became involved in the harvesting of hay, wheat, and oats. I usually was merely a tagalong or observer, but I did get to ride along on the hay wagon and help pick up shocks of wheat.

The wheat field was cut with a binder which left the wheat in small bundles in the field. Then the farmers and their hired hands would stack the bundles in little clusters. About five bundles were stacked on end in a circle to form a little teepee and two or three bundles were bent across the knee and placed on top to form a roof. When these shocks of wheat were cured and dry, they were gathered onto a farm wagon and taken to the threshing machine. I enjoyed running from shock to shock as they were pitched onto the wagon, for under each shock of bundles were snakes, toads, big spiders, mice, and other small creatures.

The threshing machine and the threshing process were truly fascinating, too. I never did understand how the threshing machine worked; straw went blowing out one pipe while clean wheat grains ran down a chute into sacks which were quickly tied and placed on another wagon. I remember the farmers stating that the threshing machine was the hungriest thing on earth; they said it ate and ate but never got full.

Jimmy, the farmer's son, built a boat that summer and placed it on the large farm pond. That was a real thrill, rowing around in the water. Behind the pond was a large woods where great blue herons had a rookery. We often saw the herons wading around in the shallow part of the pond. The pond also had turtles, bullfrogs, and other forms of aquatic life which we could observe from the boat.

My father had a garden behind our house and had transplanted some grapes and other plants from the old homestead in Colerain. One evening, while helping to catch and destroy bean beetles, I found a large American toad. I did not want to keep it penned up but did want a chance to see it again. I dug a hole in the ground, placed a wooden box over it, made a scooped-out entrance leading under the box and placed a pan of water inside on the ground. I went out the next day to see whether the toad was inside where I had left it. Sure enough, I found it sitting in the pan of water. Each evening the toad would come out and go hopping along the rows of green beans, picking off bean beetles with its lightning fast tongue. I was worried because I never saw the toad drink any water, but my father explained that toads can absorb water right through their skin and do not have to drink as people do.

If I were asked to list the experiences of that summer which are most vivid in my mind today, the list would include the following:

1. Sitting in a tomato patch eating ripe tomatoes, a tomato in one hand and a salt shaker in the other.
2. The blend of aromas around the barn in the evening—cow manure, horse manure, straw, hay, grains, and the odor of the milk house.
3. Eating an apple that tasted like a banana and was called a "banana apple."
4. Picking and eating large, dark cherries from a tree known as the "blackheart cherry."
5. Watching all the cows come into the barn for milking and noting how each turned at the proper aisle and walked to its stall.
6. The night when the aurora borealis or northern lights made the entire sky look like a bunch of opened umbrellas, side by side, with constant flickering and waves of light plus a sound like radio static in the air.
7. Picking blackberries and discovering a hornets' nest.
8. Listening to the calls of whippoorwills at night.
9. Sitting on the front porch at night, looking at car lights coming from town and trying to guess whether the car was my dad's.
10. Chasing and catching fireflies.

During the middle of the summer I heard a sound that sent chills up and down my spine—it was the buzzing, lonely call of the annual cicada or locust. I had learned that its call meant summer was drawing to an end and school days were coming again. The farmers said the singing of locusts meant just six more weeks until the first frost. I kept asking the folks how many weeks it would be before school started. In September, I entered the second grade in a one-room, red brick school.

There were eight grades in one room and one teacher taught all eight grades; each grade sat in a different row of seats. Some rows were longer than others; for instance, there were only three of us in the second grade. The school was about a quarter of a mile from our house and we walked to and from school each day. By "we" I mean my brother plus several children from neighboring farms. In the fall, we often walked through patches of sticktights or Spanish needles. Some had pretty yellow flowers and in the morning were decorated with the circular webs of spiders. These webs were especially beautiful when laden with dewdrops sparkling in the morning sunlight. When there was heavy dew, we tried to walk at the edge of the road so our shoes wouldn't get soaked. I didn't like school but did enjoy walking to and from—mostly from—school. I also enjoyed recess periods when we could go outside and play a game called "Annie over," which involved throwing a large ball over the arched roof of the school building.

Slowly I became adjusted to the routine of going to school. I managed to remain in good spirits by thinking of approaching weekends and holidays. The first holiday of the school year was Halloween.

I remember spending days shelling ears of field corn until I had a large sack of yellow and orange kernels. I enjoyed scooping these kernels up in my hands and letting them trickle back into the sack—they felt cool and slippery. We also made jack-o-lanterns in preparation for Halloween and had candles burning inside them several nights before. There was something mysterious about the blackened inside of a pumpkin—the aroma was unforgettable. The climax came on the night we went Halloweening.

A dozen or more of us would go from farm to farm, throwing shelled corn on porches and against windows. Sometimes the occupants would be hiding in bushes and would jump out and scare us or throw a shower of corn at us. Then we would be invited inside for cider, doughnuts, fudge, taffy, popcorn, and other refreshments. Everyone had a good time being tricked and playing tricks on one another.

Thanksgiving, Christmas, and Easter also had a special country flavor. Pumpkin pies were made from fresh pumpkins and spices, the roast turkey was a freshly dressed turkey full of natural flavor, and the nougat and fruit centers of chocolate Easter eggs had a better taste than those which are mass produced today.

Much of the home canning and other forms of food preservation had disappeared from our home. Most foods were purchased from stores in town and from a bakery truck that came to the house two or three times a week. World War II was well underway and my father was earning good money at his new job in a factory. Working six and seven days per week left him little time to work in his garden or with the flowers around the lawn.

In winter we walked to school as fast as we could. After walking a while into the cold winter wind, we would turn around and walk with our backs to the wind. Our faces would suddenly feel warm. When we arrived at the red brick schoolhouse, we rushed inside and huddled around a potbellied stove. During recess periods we built snowmen and snow forts and threw snowballs at one another.

As spring approached, the road to school became slushy and we had to wear boots. The snow finally melted away; warm breezes out of the south brought rain showers and a gradual warming trend which made the days seem a little brighter. By May, the air was filled with the fragrance of apple blossoms and the incessant calls of frogs.

Most of our family were homesick for the hills when summer came again. Although we lived in a rural area, the land was rather flat and monotonous. Most of it was in farmland with only a few wooded sections remaining. The difference in topography, school life, changes in home life, and other factors created a different situation. I cannot remember the experiences in that flat region so well as I can those associated with my preschool days in the hills. But there are a few pleasant memories that linger in my mind. Each is an isolated memory without the enhancement which surrounded all the experiences I had before entering the first grade in Colerain.

Memories of the school year, its weekends, and the second summer in the country north of Sebring, Ohio, include these:

1. Gathering puffballs and mushrooms in the pastures during the fall; my dad and I were about the only ones in our family who liked to eat them. I think other members of our family lost their taste for them when they learned that the largest mushrooms and puffballs often were found in a clump of old cow manure!

2. Watching the farmers butcher hogs in the winter and eating cracklings that would spill out of a large kettle onto the snow. Once I ate so many cracklings I became very sick and never have cared for them since.

3. Discovering chicken nests in the hayloft of the barn where hens had been laying their eggs; sometimes there were twenty or thirty eggs in these nests, but they weren't any good for eating.

4. Being fascinated by a glass egg that was placed under certain hens so they wouldn't feel their nests had been robbed.

5. Placing a chicken's head under its wing, swinging it back and forth and then placing it on the ground—we called this "putting a chicken to sleep." A chicken would remain in this position for a long time before pulling its head from under its wing, getting up on its feet, and walking away clucking to itself.

6. Hypnotizing a chicken; that is, laying a chicken on its side on the dusty ground while drawing a straight line out from its beak across the ground with a stick. The chicken would watch the stick and lie on the ground for a few minutes after the stick was removed. Some said the chicken was hypnotized by the line which the stick made in the dust.

7. Lying on the dark wood of our front porch on a chilly but sunny spring morning, feeling the absorbed heat of the sun.

8. Walking in our bare feet on the paved highway. It was fun to walk on the patches of tar; they were very warm and

soft as bread dough. The trick was to walk on the crust of this tar without breaking through. When the crust broke, our toes became coated with hot tar. Then pieces of grass, seeds, gravel, and sand were picked up by our sticky toes.

9. Seeing a lizard, called a "blue-tailed skink," which lived near the cistern. I was told if you opened your mouth when you were near them, lizards would jump down your throat. One day, while looking at the skink, I decided to open my mouth. The skink moved towards me and for several years I thought there was some truth to this superstition.

10. Looking for and seeing shooting stars in the night sky.

When I was about half way through the third grade, my folks moved into Sebring so that my dad could be closer to work. We lived at the edge of town, about two blocks beyond the factory where my father was employed. Sebring was primarily a pottery town with about two or three other major industries. Going to school in town, becoming acquainted with other kids who had never lived in the country, and living in a house not far from a busy factory and only a block away from a heavily-used set of railroad tracks were radical changes in my life. Unless they are of great magnitude or persist for a long time, one tends to forget the undesirable aspects of life. And, so it is—all I can remember is having had feelings of unhappiness in that new situation. However, those feelings were only temporary, for episodes of contentment and enjoyment began to unfold.

One of the happy events at the new school was digging up crawdads during recess periods. Other boys and I would find their chimneys of mud in a low, moist area next to the school and dig with a spade until we found a large crawdad—sometimes two or three feet below the surface.

The crawdads had chosen a good location, but the same was not true for the contractors' choice of a site on which to build the school. Cracks began to appear in the walls, and after several building inspectors had surveyed the situation, the building was condemned and all of us had to be transported by bus to another school building. At that time, I thought the crawdads were probably happy to see us leave. The old building was supposed to sink into the ground but I don't believe it ever did.

By being in separate grades and rooms, I didn't worry quite so much about the years ahead. I had accepted the fact that there was no way to avoid going through school, and the exposure I had had in the country school—that is, being in the same room and hearing the complicated lessons of the other grade levels— made me realize that learning was serious business. I knew each bit of learning was in preparation for something more compli- cated. So, as boring as regimented learning was, I managed to earn good grades and do what I was told. By the time I reached the fifth grade, a series of encouraging happenings had begun.

Whenever we were reading about something pertaining to a farm, I was called upon to make additiional comments. In our lessons, whenever a stream, rock, minnow, or other form of na- ture was mentioned, the lesson suddenly became more interest- ing. Many teachers, who were not nature enthusiasts, detected my interest in nature and went out of their way to offer en- couragement and guidance.

By this time I had learned to read, and the first nonclassroom book that I read was Ernest Thompson Seton's *Wild Animals I Have Known*. Seton's stories about the lives of various animals recalled many of my childhood experiences in Colerain. His de- scriptions and explanations enlightened me about many forms of nature with which I was acquainted but really did not know. This book left me feeling that Seton was truly a great, kind man.

About two weeks before Christmas, our class decided to have an exchange of gifts. Everyone put his/her name into a box and each of us drew a name. A few days later I learned from another student that my name had been drawn by a boy who came from a very poor family—some said their family was the poorest in town. I expressed my disappointment to my parents and they gave me quite a lecture on what Christmas was supposed to mean. The day before our Christmas vacation began, our teacher called our names and handed out the Christmas presents.

I remember the teacher's picking up a rather unattractive pack- age when she called my name. The present had been wrapped in a grocery sack and tied with string. Inside was a scuffed-up book. It was entitled *Aesop's Fables*. Most of the stories involved animals and morals, and it turned out to be one of the most enjoyable books I had read. The boy had given it to me because he knew of my interest in nature; he and I had dug up crawdads when we were in the third grade.

Our family always had a bird feeder of some type during the winter and early spring. Sometimes the feeder consisted of nothing more than a flat board placed on the ground or on top of the snow. It was usually loaded with bread crumbs, corn, and other grains. This is where my interest in birds had its beginning. Seeing birds presented more of a challenge than observing stationary trees and wildflowers.

I revealed my interest in birds to a substitute teacher who taught our fifth grade class for about a week. She seemed delighted with my interest and brought me a copy of a book entitled *Field Book of Wild Birds and Their Music* by F. Schuyler Mathews. This book had beautiful color plates of birds and descriptions of their habits plus notes of music which one could play on a piano to simulate their songs. The teacher told me I could keep the book, and it has remained among my most cherished possessions.

It was about this same time that I first heard the word "conservation," and it seemed like a magic term. All through school I would look at the index of each new text to see whether conservation was mentioned. If there was a chapter on conservation, I read it immediately. In those days this was usually the last chapter in the book, or one which the teacher would skip, saying we would cover it later in the year if we had enough time. Of course, it was seldom included in the regular course work.

My parents had purchased several lots adjoining our house, and these contained a large grove of black locust trees plus an abundance of wildflowers. Beyond the grove we had a vegetable garden and a flower garden. Many domestic flowers had been transplanted to our new home from our previous residence. I enjoyed planting and taking care of a small garden; I liked to plant packets of mixed flower seeds and then wait through the summer to see all the surprises. This was more fun than planting rows of zinnias, marigolds, or other flowers.

One day on my way from school I found a dead robin which

I picked up and carried home. I decided to bury it out near my flower garden. My sisters had just thrown out some old bracelets, and I took one of them and placed it around the dead bird before placing it in a wooden cheese box. Then I buried it and marked its grave with a rock. I repeated this practice with other dead animals until I had a small animal cemetery in our back yard. Then kids from all over town began bringing me dead dogs, cats, birds, rats, opossums, and many other animals for burial services in my cemetery. About the time we wound up with three dead dogs on our front porch, my parents decided to put me out of the cemetery business.

I finally joined a Boy Scout troop, and through it my interest in nature received an extra boost. My scoutmaster was not a professional naturalist, but, like so many other people, he had a special way of encouraging my interest in nature. I enjoyed our cookouts, hikes, and camping trips, especially in winter when we stayed in a log cabin on a large Scout reservation near Youngstown. We had two special natural areas in Sebring—the "North Woods" and the "South Woods." We spent a lot of time in both areas learning how to live in a natural area without destroying it. Perhaps the greatest thrill was spending a week at summer camp.

Although Boy Scout camp was somewhat regimented with certain times designated for archery, rifle shooting, swimming, crafts, and nature study, there also was ample time when we could do what we wanted to. Most of my free time was spent with the nature counselor, an older boy who had a vast knowledge of birds. He described a large black and white woodpecker with a sharp, pointed, red crest on its head—it was about the size of a crow and was known as the pileated woodpecker. I had seen pictures of this bird and became excited when Bill, the nature counselor, told me a pair of them was nesting in the Scout reservation. He detected my enthusiasm and told me if I would meet him the next morning at four o'clock, he would take me to see their nest.

I met Bill at 4:00 A.M. at his cabin; it was still dark and the birds had not yet begun to sing. We took off, hiking to a place where a swath had been cut through part of the forested area. A power line ran through this particular cleared area. Our pants-legs and shoes were soaked from the morning dew by the time we reached the swath. The morning sun had come up enough to send shafts of light through the trees down across the open area, and birds were singing everywhere. We crawled up behind a large stump and waited. Soon the majestic pileated woodpecker came swooping across the swath and landed against the trunk of a tree about twenty yards away. Bill carefully focused his binoculars on the bird and told me to take a look.

As I watched the bird through the binoculars, I saw it move up the trunk to a hole. Then I saw three little heads sticking out of the hole; the parent woodpecker stuck its beak into the opened beak of one of the young and then flew away. Then from another direction came the other parent and repeated the process. Bill said we should not go any closer, for we might disturb them. So we slowly retreated into the woods and returned to our cabins in time for breakfast.

Bill taught me the calls of many birds during that week—the buzzy call of the blue-winged warbler, the clucking call of the cuckoo, the calls of redstarts, tanagers, thrushes, and many others. Some of these I had heard before but had not known by name.

At this same time I heard about a man, called a naturalist, who worked in a large park. He also wrote an interesting column in the Sunday newspaper; it seemed as though he spent a lot of time keeping tabs on happenings in the fields and forests. I wondered if I might someday have such a job. Close friends and relatives said it was a possibility. Teachers advised that such jobs were very scarce, didn't pay much money, and would probably require a college degree. By the time I reached the seventh grade, I knew I wanted to be a naturalist but worried about having to go to college.

When I entered high school, I decided to take a college preparatory course. I had acquired a reputation as a "nature nut" and received a lot of teasing from my classmates and teachers. But it was all in fun, for whenever I would ask them if I should go into some other type of work, they'd turn around and give me all kinds of reasons for staying with nature. I was called "bird brain," "buggy," "nature boy," and a few would give out horse laughs when they remarked that "our nature boy has bats in his belfry" or "Paul, here, will be studying the birds and the bees."

While working on the signaling merit badge in the Boy Scouts I had as my merit-badge counselor the man who ran the Western Union telegraph station. When he learned of my interest in nature, he suggested that I meet his son who was a close friend of Don Eckelberry, an artist who was receiving nationwide recognition for his outstanding bird paintings. So I met Ray Crewson, who had served in World War II in the United States Air Force. Ray had been shot down several times on missions over Germany; he had been captured on his last one and had spent some time in a concentration camp before the war ended. He and Don had been friends for many years in Sebring and Ray arranged for me to meet Don when he was visiting in Sebring. At that time, Don lived in Chagrin Falls, Ohio, near Cleveland. He invited me up for a weekend I will never forget.

In a letter Don told me to come by bus to the Cleveland bus terminal where I would be met and transported to his home. His studio was in his home; it overlooked a beautiful ravine. That night I was entertained by the sounds of flying squirrels landing on the roof. Early the next morning we began our birding expedition. We saw more than a hundred different species of birds in that one day.

One of the areas we visited was Mosquito Reservoir near Warren, Ohio. On the mud flats we saw all kinds of beautiful shorebirds. Don had hoped to show me the rare buff-breasted sandpiper, but we didn't have any luck. We went through a field clapping our hands and scared up several short-eared owls. It was interesting to learn that this type of owl nested on the ground. The last bird of the day was a barred owl which lived in the ravine near Don's home.

Don stood at the upper end of the ravine and began hooting like a barred owl. Soon an owl began to answer. Then we saw the huge bird flying up the ravine toward us. It landed in a tree right above us and gave us the craziest look before taking off!

Don gave me his personal records of bird trips he had made as a high school boy around Sebring. They were checklists of species and accounts of where they had been seen. Through them I learned where and when to look for various species.

As busy as he was with his paintings and illustrating of numerous books, Don would take time to write to me and offer advice. He would also confirm certain sightings about which I was uncertain. Knowing this great artist and having him autograph several books which he had illustrated were definite incentives towards my pursuing a career as a naturalist.

In my junior year of high school, I managed to get a part-time job in a service station. I washed cars, pumped gas, changed tires, fixed flats, and performed many of the other duties associated with service stations. Our busiest days were on the weekends and when spring rolled around, I felt the urge to ride my bicycle to the small lakes and ponds about twenty miles from town in order to see all the ducks and other waterfowl which were returning or passing through. When I asked the owner if I could have a Saturday or Sunday off in order to see the migrating birds, he said it could not be arranged because those were our busiest days. I always felt, however, that if I had wanted off to play football or baseball, something would have been arranged. But to look at a bunch of birds?—How ridiculous!

My parents suggested that I approach the high school superintendent and ask if he would excuse me from school during one of the week days when I didn't have to report to the service station. I was scared to death of our superintendent but finally got up enough nerve to step into his office one morning before classes had begun.

My knees were shaking and the palms of my hands were wet with perspiration as I asked the superintendent if I might be excused from school for a day. When he asked why I wanted to be excused, I just knew a negative reply would be forthcoming. After I had told him I wanted to see the ducks that came through there only during the spring, he didn't give me an answer but went to look at my school records. I remember his looking up at me and saying, "You really want to see those ducks, don't you?"

After I described how beautiful ducks were at that time of year, he closed the folder which contained my records, looked at me, and said, "I hate to see you spoil a perfect attendance record, but if those ducks mean that much to you, we'll see to it that you're excused for that day."

Later in the spring, the superintendent stopped me in the hall and asked about the ducks. I do believe he realized I gained something from that experience that I couldn't have gained in the classroom. The next year I was excused again for the same purpose.

Although I played football, softball, baseball, and other games with boys in my neighborhood, I could never persuade any of them to go on any bird hikes with me. Consequently, most of my discoveries in natural areas were shared with no one. All I could do was tell a few willing listeners about the showy orchis, beavers, blue goose, loon, and other forms of nature I had seen. When I learned that naturalists led interested people on nature walks, I was further encouraged to be a naturalist.

I rode my bicycle and hiked around the countryside every time I had the opportunity. I heard sounds I could not identify and saw many plants or wildflowers which remained mysteries. But this was part of the fun. I gradually accumulated books on identification and if my curiosity was aroused enough, I'd spend hours leafing through a particular book until I was able to run down a mystery plant or bird. Who cared whether I knew the names of everything I enjoyed? I wasn't being tested or graded during my outdoor adventures.

There were many other people and events which played significant roles in my choosing a career as a naturalist; if I were to describe all of them, this entire book would be an autobiography. There is one more experience, however, that I'd like to describe, for it illustrates several aspects of nature and human nature.

While walking to school one day during my senior year, I was talking to some other boys. One of them said something that reminded me of a dream or a similar situation. But when I tried to recall the entire situation I was reminded of, I couldn't quite put it all together and experienced a strange feeling. After a month or so this phenomenon recurred. I told my parents there were times when I couldn't remember things I was trying to remember and experienced funny feelings. It was a feeling difficult to describe and my parents merely replied that they forgot a lot of things, too.

Feelings of confusion became more frequent as the school year progressed. I didn't know what was wrong and began asking other students if they had such experiences. One boy remarked, "Hell, man! I feel like that all the time!" It finally reached a stage where another person would notice a vacant stare in my eyes during one of these strange episodes. If someone asked me a question while I was experiencing one of these weird feelings, he would receive an answer completely irrelevant to his question.

My parents took me to see our family doctor, who immediately diagnosed my condition as petit mal, a mild form of epilepsy. Petit mal didn't sound so bad, but when the doctor used the term *epilepsy*, it seemed as if the whole world collapsed. He noticed the shocked expressions on our faces and said, "Now, hold on there—this isn't the end of the world."

The doctor said he was not up on the latest form of treatment for this disorder but knew that even the most severe forms could be completely controlled. He said I would have to go to a certain clinic in order to receive the proper therapy. Then I asked him if this would interfere with my going to college. He asked where I intended to go. When I mentioned Ohio State University, he smiled and told me I could forget about the clinic he had mentioned; he explained that the Ohio State University had the most advanced program of treatment in the entire state.

We always respected our family doctor's honesty; if he didn't know something, he would admit it and recommend someone else. Therefore, we had faith in him when he said he did know something. And we took his advice when he said not to keep this a secret or hush-hush type of thing, but to tell people exactly what the ailment was. He gave me some medication which helped me but didn't completely halt the seizures. This was a period of great confusion.

People were telling me I should go into engineering or some type of work where I'd be inside. One man said, "Listen, I like the birds, too—I feed them in the winter, but they don't feed me. They're not going to keep meat and potatoes on your table." Then there were those who said I should go to a small college and that I'd merely be a number at a large university like Ohio State. Perhaps the most helpful, sincere bit of advice was that offered by my homeroom teacher who also had been my math instructor all through high school.

I had been what was then called an honor student and had taken two years of algebra, plane geometry, solid geometry, trigonometry, and physics. I asked my instructor if he thought I should try to take an engineering course in college. He said he thought I could make the grades but didn't think I'd ever be happy as an engineer. I remember his saying, "Why don't you stick with your nature studies? That's what you're really cut out for."

During that summer I had to make a decision. I wanted to go to Ohio State because of the hope it offered in controlling the seizures which still bothered me. Then, too, Ohio State offered courses which seemed to be more in line with nature studies. Yet I was afraid of the bigness of such a university. After touring the campus with a friend, I decided that I could cope with its size. That fall I entered college at Ohio State.

After I had taken the entrance physical and showed the doctor in charge a note from my doctor, arrangements were made for me to see a neurologist at the Student Health Center. I was introduced to a new form of medication and arrangements were made for a brain wave test or electroencephalogram. Later I took another EEG to confirm the findings of the first one.

The neurologist gradually increased the dosage of medication. I remember having made it through a complete day without a sign of a seizure. Then I began counting the days—two, three, four, five, six and a whole week. Then, two weeks, three weeks, and an entire month without a sign. The neurologist was pleased and said, "I think we've hit the magic number now. But don't go out and celebrate yet!"

After a year had passed without any seizures or inklings of seizures, the neurologist told me he thought we had it completely licked. Then he looked up from his desk, wrung his hands and said, "All we need now is a pill to give the public to get them to understand what this stuff is all about—that's our major problem."

While I've encountered a few people who are prejudiced and have false notions about epilepsy, I've known a countless number who have been extremely broadminded and understanding about this matter. I learned that people weren't stupid and could readily understand things if they were explained to them. I simply told them the truth—that November 23, 1952, was the last time I was bothered by this disorder. I was turned down on more than thirty jobs when I graduated from college because of this medical record. So, I know what prejudice based upon ignorance amounts to. But this doesn't blot out all the people who were willing to look at the facts. Out of my brief period of worry and discomfort I do believe I gained some understanding of those who have more severe afflictions and problems. Nature had been a great help to me during this trying period and I knew it could also help others.

I knew nature held no prejudices against anyone, and working with a variety of people in the out-of-doors should help erase my own prejudices. I also knew that experiences in nature would give a person a certain stability to withstand many of life's pressures and frustrations. Now, after having worked as an interpretive naturalist for more than twenty-two years, I have no doubts about the values one can derive from working and sharing with others in the out-of-doors. I hope the remainder of this book will open a new world to you or will help show you how to open it to others.

Nature Interpretation

Is Common Sense

It would be easy for you who read this to say that I'm guilty of being narrow-minded. By this I mean one could assume I've considered everything I experienced as a child as being the best experiences for children of today. In many respects, like many other adults, I am guilty of regarding many changes or differences in behavior as being wrong. But here, I am talking about a unique subject—nature. And for the most part, nature and natural laws have not changed through the years.

I would not expect the songs which I enjoyed as a youngster to be received and liked by the children of today. The same holds true for the types of clothing, shoes, toys, perfumes, cars, and certain customs which have changed through the years. But the many forms of nature which thrilled me as a child continue to thrill today's children.

In giving talks to various groups, I have often mentioned some of the experiences with nature which I described in the preceding chapter. I have noticed smiles on faces; I've seen some people begin to nod their heads in agreement. Later, they have come up to me and have told me how certain descriptions reminded them of similar experiences which they had temporarily forgotten. I hope you have been able to relate to some of the experiences I described. It should be apparent how important it is for kids to have experiences they will enjoy remembering throughout their lives. But why should these experiences involve nature?

It is significant that I can remember so many forms of nature around my childhood home. It's even more significant that I can't remember much about furnishings in the house, my father's car, toys I probably played with, and other manufactured items. I know there was linoleum on the kitchen floor, but I can't remember its color or whether it contained a pattern. I know we ate at a large table, but I can't remember what it looked like. Neither can I remember the appearance of dinner plates, tablecloths, carpets, kitchen appliances, or furniture. Why is this?

Spearmint, frogs, insects, and other forms of nature have remained essentially the same as they were back in the 1930s. With nature a person can experience the same sights, sounds, aromas, and other sensations from year to year. Artificial items constantly change; there is little about modern vehicles or appliances to remind us of those existing fifty years ago. It's comforting to know that some things are the same today as they were fifty years ago; it's comforting to know they'll probably be the same fifty or a hundred years from today.

Sensations and feelings associated with nature are aesthetic qualities. I think aesthetic qualities make lasting impressions upon the human mind. Music is something aesthetic and I've had an experience with music which serves as a good illustration.

I have accumulated a large collection of long-play phonograph records. Although most of these contain six selections on each side, there usually are only two or three appealing selections on each record. Rather than place the needle on my favorite bands and risk scratching various records, I let them play from beginning to end. Sometimes I want to hear a certain selection on a record I haven't played for a year or more. When I place it on the phonograph I become aware of a fascinating phenomenon.

Although I cannot remember the names of all the selections or what order they are in, when one selection ends, I immediately know what is coming next. It's like hearing the beginning of a composition before any sound is produced. If you have listened to many records repeatedly, I'm sure you have had the same experience. This illustrates how the music, itself, rather than the names of the selections makes a lasting impression upon our minds.

Sights, sounds, aromas, and other sensations experienced by children while having an enjoyable time in the out-of-doors are aesthetic and will leave permanent impressions upon their minds. These are real experiences; words, photographs, slide presentations, movies, recordings of natural sounds, and other audiovisuals are inadequate substitutes—maybe better than nothing, but not the same as the real experience.

You probably have noticed how much easier it is to remember a melody from a new selection than the words which accompany it. This also applies to nature walks where youngsters experience melodies as well as words. A melody in nature involves the freshness of the air in a woods, calls of birds and frogs, beautiful colors of wildflowers, and a variety of intangible feelings. These will be remembered whereas factual information pertaining to various natural phenomena may be quickly forgotten.

Words about nature are rather meaningless to those who have never experienced the natural phenomena referred to. It is difficult, for example, to describe the aroma of bergamot. And how would you describe the taste of a banana to one who has never tasted one? No matter how much a person learns about a banana, it won't have much real meaning until he actually tastes, smells, sees, and feels a real banana.

Have you and the children close to you ever tasted pawpaws, persimmons, May apples, wintergreen berries, or butternuts? Have you sniffed the aroma of sweet cicely, pineapple weed, fruits of prickly ash, an osage orange, or the crushed seeds of yarrow? How important are such experiences? If nothing else, they are broadening.

Foods do not all taste alike and I don't think they were meant to taste alike. Wouldn't it be dull if all vegetables tasted like carrots, all meats like ham, all fruits like apples, and all beverages like lemonade? Would a picture of a sirloin steak on a grill be any more appealing than one of a wiener if they tasted alike or if a person had never tasted either? When children's or adults' experiences are limited to the world of audio-visuals, all phenomena might as well taste, smell, and feel alike. Just as there is a value in knowing from past experience that a meal will be a combination of many tastes, there is also a value in knowing from experience that the fields, woodlands, and other outdoor areas hold a variety of sensations.

Few would dispute the notion that new and pleasant sensations are good for the human mind. Some of the greatest poets and composers were inspired by nature which is reflected in many of their works. Nature is both a stimulant and a tranquilizer; I like to think of nature as a source of vitamins for the mind. As nature stimulates and soothes the mind, it also nourishes our deepest thoughts. Like other vitamins, these are vital to children; they cannot be obtained from a diet of asphalt and concrete.

Consider children living in the heart of some big city during the winter. You tell them spring is on its way, but what does this mean to them? What thoughts will cross their minds?

Once I heard a speaker relate a story about city children's thinking of spring as that time of year when the tar began to bubble on the roof. This might not be so bad if they could depend upon it, but that roof might be there and it might not. It could be replaced by a different roof on a different building. Their sidewalk might be torn up and the street widened so people can reach shopping centers more rapidly. Playmates across the street might be gone—moved to another city. And kids might find themselves in a different city where all people are strangers. Buses might be running or drivers might be out on strike; school might be in session or teachers might be out of work; public officials might be regarded as honest and upright or there might be scandals in the newspapers; parents might be together or they might be separated or divorced. Changes and adjustments in our modern lives are endless.

Comparing all this to a long-play record, let's say the children are listening to the winter band. When it ends, will they sense what's coming on the spring band before it begins to play? Will it be the same as it was last spring? If it has been different every spring for the past ten years, will the children anticipate anything other than change itself?

Consider children who have been introduced to nature through repeated visits to the winter fields and woodlands. They have felt snowflakes on their faces; they have had fun following rabbit tracks in the snow; they have seen many winter birds and know certain fungi thrive and many plants remain green throughout the winter. Although they may live in a city and be exposed to problems of everyday city life, they also know there is a place where pleasant experiences can be enjoyed. It's doubly important if these same children have been exposed to the spring fields and woodlands.

Think of the youngster who gets out in the world of nature from the time maple sap begins to run and ducks and geese begin moving north, to the time when spring wildflowers begin pushing up through the leaves on the forest floor and tree buds begin to burst. He has tasted wintergreen leaves and fruits; he has sniffed the fragrance of a scraped twig of sassafras or red-osier dogwood; has squeezed the seed head of bergamot and has inhaled its invigorating fragrance; has felt the fuzzy leaves of mullein; has heard the first calls of spring peepers and chorus frogs; or has simply experienced the feelings of being in the out-of-doors during the spring. Place this child in the situation of experiencing the winter band of our imaginary record.

In the first place the winter band will not be that unpleasant. When this band ends, the child will detect what's coming next. And what's more important, it will be there!

A person well saturated with experiences in nature won't feel too uncomfortable at any season because he knows there is a place where beauty, harmony, and interrelatedness exist. Being fully aware of this fact alone is comforting to the mind. Being aware of nature's reliability is even more comforting. I first became aware of this after working with a group of emotionally disturbed children.

It was during the summer and I had stopped to show the group a sassafras tree. They seemed interested in the fact that this tree contained four different shapes of leaves. I picked a leaf, scraped its stem and told the youngsters to pass it around and smell it. All of them were intrigued by its strong lemon aroma. One of the youngsters asked if all sassafras leaves would smell like that. I told him I had never found any that didn't. They would go to a leaf and ask, "Is this a sassafras?" After I had confirmed their identification, they would give the leaf the nose test. They did this with numerous sassafras trees during the remainder of our walk. They seemed to get happier and happier each time they tried a new sassafras leaf and one might have imagined the leaves were having some type of narcotic effect. I didn't capitalize on the situation at that moment, for I wasn't aware of its significance.

The following day I was leading several school groups on nature walks and observed that they, too, were intrigued by various aromatic plants. Then it hit me—these kids were fascinated by the fact that they had discovered something which was as it was supposed to be. After that I began to take advantage of the situation; the pitch went something like this:

"This plant has this aroma today and it had this same aroma yesterday and probably a thousand years ago. If this species can survive, it will have the same aroma a thousand years from now. And it will smell this way for you whether you're first or last in your class, tall or short, male or female, black or white, wealthy or poor, lucky or unlucky. Like most things in nature, this is something you can count on."

In view of all the monotony and frustration of everyday life, created and controlled by man, there is a value in knowing from real experience that something is dependable without being monotonous. All the leaves on sassafras, for example, yield the same aroma but no two leaves are identical. In the midst of nature's complexities there are many laws and principles which hold true.

Man's world is inconsistent, presenting a picture of constant change as well as one of monotony. Certain makes of automobiles are all alike one year but have to be different the next. Dishes, cups, and many other objects are produced by the thousands, out of identical molds. A performer will sell a million identical records, but the recordings soon will be considered unpopular and he will have to make new and different ones in a different style. In our world we see much sameness which has to change by tomorrow; in nature we see a great variety of appearances with properties that hold true.

If people can be exposed repeatedly to the natural world, they will accumulate a built-in or recorded stability which can help them overcome anxieties, hypocrisies, and all types of boredom. When things become distressing, they can turn on their recordings of pleasant, assuring experiences and drown out the unpleasantness of everyday life.

I have heard it said that today's children really don't need any exposure to nature, that they are unaware of nature and, therefore, do not know what they're missing. Of course, many children and adults as well don't know what they're missing, but neither are they acquiring a set of values to help them overcome various problems. One who has never tasted certain basic foods doesn't know what he's missing, either. This, however, doesn't mean that his body doesn't need them.

Nature's manner of being completely and absolutely nondiscriminatory towards people, plus its ability to soothe and strengthen the mind, have paradoxically turned some people away. Movies, radio, and television often have portrayed the nature enthusiast as an eccentric, odd-acting, or odd-looking person. I have heard it said that many nature enthusiasts have serious emotional problems. Now just for the sake of a little controversy, let's suppose that such people are emotionally unbalanced. Should this turn others away from nature? Haven't many looked at this the wrong way?

Those finding pleasure through a kinship with nature are not bothering their neighbors or creating disturbances. Indeed, maybe a few people are getting the help they need in order to overcome mental or emotional problems. Such persons could not be in better hands and they deserve a pat on the back rather than ridicule. Some people, who do not meet certain standards laid down by the majority, are excluded from certain social circles and organizations. But nature will treat them the same as it treats all others.

So avoiding nature because one believes odd persons enjoy it is like avoiding those foods which have been prescribed for an anemic person or avoiding seeing a doctor for needed advice because he treated someone with a serious illness. Thanks to some of our modern entertainers and highly respected personalities who have voiced an interest in nature, many people are getting rid of this old stigma.

Each decade sees more and more children robbed of the opportunity to commune with nature. Now it is time to use the automobile and other forms of transportation, which have created many of our problems, as means of taking more people more often to the fields and woodlands. Like needles on broken records these vehicles go over the same bands day after day. Let's move on to some new bands where all of us can enjoy new sensations, values, and rewards. It is time to give serious thought to nature interpretation as a simple activity which is open to all.

Once I was leading a group of school children on a walk near a small pond. It was in May and the water was full of tadpoles or pollywogs. Near the bank I spotted a large tadpole, stooped down and pointed toward it. Each of the thirty children wanted to get a good look and converged on the spot. I felt a hand on my shoulder as one of the youngsters held on and peered down into the water. Soon there were other hands on my other shoulder. One of the kids said, "Gee! Is that ever a big one!"

Then there was a lot of pushing as the youngsters piled up behind me. Finally, I couldn't withstand their combined weight and wound up in the pond along with five of the children.

While this experience seems humorous to many adults, they fail to realize its true significance. Common sense should tell all parents and teachers the children's excitement didn't result from my presence; it resulted from the tadpole's appearance. All parents should know they could show a tadpole to their own children under more favorable circumstances; that is, without thirty children competing for a view. And it should be apparent how starved children are for some of the most common, easily-found phenomena.

Do you remember the "big rock" I described in the first chapter? It must have been about ten years later that I visited the old homestead with some of my relatives. I just had to see the big rock again. When I walked down along the creek and came to the big rock, I was disappointed. It had shrunk and was merely a good-sized stone or small boulder. I also noticed that the hill had shrunk; it didn't take long to reach the creek. And the creek, itself, had dried up through the years; it was only about two feet wide and I could step across it. My parents and others, who had reached adulthood at the time I was a child, assured me that everything was the same as it was when we lived there ten years or so before. Things had not shrunk; I had grown up. This taught me a good lesson which I try to keep in mind whenever I'm working with children in the out-of-doors.

I know I have to try to see things through the eyes of the children. Experience and common sense tell me a large stone is a giant boulder to a child; a small grove of trees is a forest; a puddle is a pond. Things they are seeing for the first time are fresher, fuzzier, smoother and more amazing than they might be to me or other adults. The children find caterpillars, beetles, bugs, and other small creatures which my eyes might pass over. The children are my hand lens. Let them be yours. Being smaller, children take a liking to small animals. They see much that we adults miss because their eyes are closer to the ground—they are more down-to-earth.

How many preschool children do you know of who have opportunities to visit a clean creek, a woods, an open field, or other natural area whenever they want to? If a child doesn't see a woods until he's ten years of age, which is the case with about half the city children I work with, think what he has missed. He hasn't merely missed seeing a woods, a situation which some think has been corrected after he has seen one. Such a child has missed seeing a woods at three, four, five, six, seven, eight, and nine years of age! He/she will never know the feelings to be experienced at those different ages. Just think how much so many children are being cheated out of. And think how much we are missing by not witnessing the great variety of remarks, gestures, facial expressions, and other reactions of all those different-aged children.

I used the woods only as an example—the relationships between all natural phenomena and children are different at various age levels. A toad or turtle arouses different feelings in a three-year-old from those it arouses in a five-year-old. Children have an instinctive affinity for all types of life but this gradually fades away as they grow older if it isn't nourished. This might be compared to small babies being able to swim by instinct, but if they aren't introduced to water until they are older, swimming doesn't come to them as easily.

I have noticed children's reactions to a wide variety of natural phenomena on numerous occasions. One of the more significant of these has been their reactions to dead logs and trees.

Many naturalists throughout the land spend considerable time and effort explaining to people why various natural parks have not been cleared of logs, dead elms, and brush. After they go to great lengths to explain how dead logs and trees play vital roles in the forest community, they usually are told, "Well, there might be some truth in that, but I still think the place looks a mess."

The type of complaint I usually receive over the phone goes something like this:

"I'm a taxpayer and I have a complaint to make about all the trash out in 'your' parks."

I ask, "Did you see a lot of bottles, tin cans, or paper along the trails or do you mean the picnic areas were badly littered?"

The caller replies, "No! No! I'm talking about all those dead logs left lying around in the woods. Why don't you clean those parks up and make them look like something?"

I feel like a tape recorder as I go through a routine explanation at the end of which the caller either hangs up on me or says, "I still think if 'your' parks are for people they ought to be made presentable to people."

Then about the time I begin wondering whether our natural areas really have any chance of surviving in the midst of so much criticism, I find myself leading a group of school children along a nature trail. When we come within view of a huge log that was once a large oak tree, the children are drawn to it. As they race around looking at the types of fungi, mosses, insect holes, half-eaten acorns, etc., I interrupt them and tell them I want to ask a question. Again, I feel like a tape recorder as I go through the following routine:

I say, "You see this big log lying here and all those other logs lying around back there in the woods?" As the children nod their heads and look around, I continue, "A lot of people tell us it would be a good idea if we'd take all these logs out of here, clean out all those dead elm trees that stick out like sore thumbs, get on the ball and make this park really look like something nice. Don't you think that would be a good idea?"

Usually, there's a spontaneous and emphatic *no* from the group, or they stand there and shake their heads. Then I ask them why they don't agree.

Even though the youngsters may be only six, seven, or eight years of age, they give some good reasons for leaving dead logs and trees in a natural area. The remarks from such children are reassuring: I find myself leaning back against the dead log, saying to myself, "Keep it coming, children—please keep it coming!"

I can't remember every remark the children—the little messengers of hope—have made. But the ones that continue to ring in my ears include these:

1. "That's what we came here to see!"
2. "It wouldn't be as pretty without the logs!"
3. "It wouldn't be a woods!"
4. "Nature put them here!"
5. "It wouldn't be nature!"
6. "Where would all the animals live?"
7. "They're part of the woods, aren't they?"
8. "They're nice!"

If you have any doubt about the validity of such an experience, I'd advise you to stop reading at this point and find time to take your children, your relatives' children, or your neighbors' children to a natural woods. Lead them to a fallen tree or dead log and let them examine it thoroughly. Roll back a log and let the kids feel the coolness under it; let them see the land snails, sowbugs, centipedes, tunnels of mice and shrews, and other signs of life under the log. Then ask these children if they think the woods should be "cleaned up" by removing all the dead logs and trees. I'm confident that they will give you the right answers. And as you continue reading these pages, you'll feel more certain they aren't merely a bunch of pipe dreams or phony theories but revelations of real experiences and tested techniques.

The big puzzler for me was trying to determine how these children knew the values of dead trees. Their teachers and leaders told me they had not been taught such concepts. I believe it was instinct and extremely meaningful. It made me think about many natural concepts.

I began thinking about some of the experiences described in the first chapter; namely, the old homestead in Colerain and my Uncle Tom's farm. I had two drastically different experiences in visiting the two sites many years later.

Although the creek, big rock, and other natural features around the old homestead had shrunk through the years, the house I lived in as a child—the house where I began to develop— seemed about the same. It had been well taken care of; it was clean, coated with fresh paint, the lawn was mowed and many domestic flowers continued to thrive around it. It was a good feeling, knowing someone had taken good care of the house. The same, however, was not true when we went by the site of my Uncle Tom's farm.

The old lane leading back to this farm was gone. There were large piles of earth and rocks where the fields, woods, barn, chicken coop, and house had been. The land had been strip-mined, and I learned that the farm house and all the farm build-ings had been burned down before the land was torn to pieces by giant coal shovels. I was disappointed. I wished I had not seen what had happened and I never cared to return. But I did stop by the old homestead in Colerain several years ago on my way home from a meeting in Wheeling, West Virginia. And that was an experience never to be forgotten.

A friend and I had left Wheeling early on a Sunday morning. My friend was driving and I asked him if he'd mind going a little way off the main route so I could see the old homestead and go through Colerain once again. In less than an hour we pulled up in front of the house. The sun was shining brightly and everything seemed to sparkle with freshness and happiness. I was content to see the house and didn't get out of the car. My friend said, "Well, have you looked at it long enough?" I knew we had a long way to travel and agreed we had better continue our return trip. As we were driving up toward the little com-munity of Colerain, however, I thought I heard a familiar sound and rolled down the window.

Down through the little valley I could hear the ringing of a church bell, the same one that had rung when other children and I walked up the same road many years before on our way to Sunday school. The brightness and crispness of the morning air plus the clanging of the large bell echoing through the valley overwhelmed me with nostalgia. To my friend, all this was mere-ly a pleasant experience. The homestead, the church bell, and later, seeing children in brightly colored Sunday clothes hur-rying toward the church were pleasing to my friend's eyes. But to me they were a priceless heritage which recalled the most meaningful and enjoyable events in my early years of devel-opment. I was grateful that these things were the same as they had once been, that they had not been modernized beyond recognition. I experience similar intangible feelings when I see the looks in children's eyes and the expressions on their faces when they are in natural areas. Is it any wonder?

Whether we're thinking of the ocean waters, mountains, or other land forms, this earth is our heritage—this is where the human race had its beginning. And when man first appeared on this earth, nothing had been disturbed by man—everything was natural. Forests, fields, prairies, marshes, swamps, bogs, sand dunes, plus millions of plants and animals probably preceded man's coming into being on this earth. Children, possessing greater instinctive qualities, therefore have a greater sensitivity, understanding, and appreciation in regard to undisturbed natural areas. They still possess a feeling of closeness to their heritage. Their instinctive feelings result in their looking at a natural area and accepting everything in it for what it is. And maybe they realize how senseless it is to keep changing and destroying all the forms of nature which must have contributed in some way toward making our survival possible. By working with children in the out-of-doors, we can regain or relearn valuable concepts which will enable us to derive more enjoyment from that part of our heritage which has not been destroyed.

Sometimes it is difficult to explain what we mean by aesthetics and intangible feelings in nature. Basically, they are feelings derived from the beauty and wonder of natural phenomena. Such feelings comprise the most important aspects of nature interpretation. It would be difficult, for example, to interpret a recording of a beautiful musical composition in terms of the chemistry of the phonograph record upon which it has been recorded. Or we might marvel at a beautiful bouquet of flowers on a table and a log burning in a fireplace. When we discover that the flowers are made of plastic and that the log is made of a ceramic material fed by an artificial gas flame, something is lost. Although we cannot place a monetary value on most natural phenomena, they still have a value which we call aesthetic or intangible.

While working with some groups it is not enough to talk about the beauty, harmony, or interrelatedness of nature. One sometimes has to emphasize how plants and animals directly benefit people. While the aesthetic side of nature is quite valuable to people, there are many who do not become aware of this until they learn to appreciate the practical aspects of many plants and animals. This generally is more true of adult groups.

Of course, as one matures, he has more to be concerned about. Holding a job, providing for a family, spending money properly, and all kinds of health problems do not worry a child so much as they do an adult. Therefore, we become more conscious about money, foods for proper nutrition, clothes to wear, medicines, and other necessities of life. Even in natural areas we find ourselves looking at various phenomena in terms of dollars and cents, food value, or medicinal properties. We window-shop in the fields and woodlands just as we do in the city. Often, if something has no monetary value, isn't good to eat, and has no other value to people, we wonder what good it could possibly be.

In a park where I once worked as a naturalist we had a pet woodchuck as part of our live animal display. Children would run up to its pen and remark about all its actions. Many adults would stand by the woodchuck's pen and describe various ways to cook a woodchuck which they usually called a groundhog. I thought it was rather humorous the way our woodchuck would suddenly quit chewing on a carrot and, with a questioning expression on its face, look directly at someone who was saying something like, "The best way to fix a goundhog is to soak it in vinegar for a day or two." Our woodchuck got "butchered" so many times we finally named him "Butch."

Those who talked about eating the groundhog did so because it was the only way they had of relating to the situation. In many instances the remarks came from people who had never seen a groundhog, either in the wild or in the oven. But they had heard about groundhogs during cooking or eating conversations. There also were those who approached the woodchuck and said, "Those things can really whistle," or "My uncle had a lot of those on his farm."

People tend to relate to natural phenomena as they best know how, and this usually depends upon past experiences. Most of us are more wrapped up in practical rather than asethetic experiences in our daily lives. Although there are numerous relationships between people and the plants and animals which surround them, many remain unaware of such relationships. This is where nature interpreters can provide an invaluable service.

Let's begin right outside your classroom or home. One of the first things we see is grass. To most people grass is something green that makes an attractive lawn—something to be planted and then periodically mowed. How many realize how important the grasses are and have been to the human race?

Corn is a grass. If we didn't have it, we would have no corn bread, corn oil, corn on the cob, popcorn, or any of the other products which come from this large member of the grass family. Each day many of us eat a valuable product of another important grass—sugar cane. And children who like molasses cookies should feel an association with the grasses since certain types of molasses are obtained from sorghum. We also should mention all the cereals, breads, and other food products obtained from rice, barley, wheat, oats, rye, millet, and other grasses.

The periwinkle or common myrtle has been planted around many city homes and various buildings as a ground cover. Within the past thirty years a drug was discovered in a species of *Vinca*, the generic name of the periwinkle. The drug was named "vincristine." It reportedly has been used with a degree of success in treating certain forms of childhood leukemia. People should be reminded that this species was on this earth thousands of years before man made such a discovery. Should any plant be regarded as worthless? Do we know everything there is to know about any plant? We often have to remind people that we are not trying to save natural areas because of all the things we know about them but because of all the things we do not know about them.

Gradually an appreciation of various natural phenomena begins to unfold. The grass under one's feet, the tree towering above the sidewalk, insects visiting the flowers, and life, itself, will become more meaningful and beautiful. So, beginning with the practical we arrive at the aesthetic.

It seems that the aesthetic values in nature help to bring about the more practical rewards of nature. Generally, those phenomena which are most beautiful tend to be the most useful. It is as though beauty is an enticement for people to keep things as they are. If someone destroys the beautiful spring blossoms in an apple orchard, he will have no apples to eat later in the summer or fall. A beautiful clean river offers opportunities for fishing, swimming, canoeing, and other activities. A polluted river loses its beauty and its practicality. It does little good, however, to talk about beauty around those who have not experienced such beauty.

In the future, we will be talking and working with more and more people in city-type surroundings. Instead of describing places and phenomena with which they are unfamiliar, we can provide a greater service by talking about the forms of life which live near them or by relating other natural phenomena to those foods, medicines, clothes, and other items which are a part of their everyday lives. This type of approach is not necessary for all people; there are many in the city and country who can appreciate nature for what it is. But there are large groups of people we have not been reaching because we cannot find a common ground for communication. The practical approach to nature interpretation might remedy this situation.

A shameful tragedy and one which greatly disturbs me is the way so many people have been led into believing that one has to know the names of all the plants and animals in the out-of-doors in order to take children on enjoyable, meaningful excursions through the fields and woodlands. The naming, cataloguing, and categorizing of natural phenomena are important in the field of research. In academic education, they also have their place—for the sake of communication, if for no other reason. It's easier to give the name of something which someone else knows by name than it is to give a complete description which someone else knows by description. Naming might have its rightful place, but this place is not in the out-of-doors with children to whom names, for the most part, are meaningless and quickly forgotten. When I say "naming" I'm talking about naming, exclusively. Let me explain what probably appears as double-talk at this point.

When I was in college, I took a course in tree identification. I learned that a tree with "opposite, pinnately compound leaves, each containing five to eleven leaflets, and having square twigs" is a blue ash. Then we went on to learn the white, red, black, green, and other ashes. Several years after I was out of college I learned that the blue ash is so called because its inner bark yields a blue dye. I also learned that if I scraped some of its twigs with my fingernail and stirred the twigs around in a glass of water, the water would take on a bluish tint. The college course had been strictly identification; nothing had been mentioned about how the tree received its name and no one seemed to give any thought to this matter. Youngsters, of course, are intrigued by the fact that twigs are able to turn water blue. Admittedly, I have to know how to identify a blue ash in order to conduct this experiment, but what I do is more important than merely teaching others how to identify the tree by its leaf arrangement and structure. Names, therefore, are like tools, but they can be dangerous tools if not used properly and carefully. It's better not to have any of these tools than to use them improperly.

The first-grade teacher I mentioned in chapter one didn't use any names but she did take us into the out-of-doors and permitted us to discover things. If the teacher had said, "Today, children, we are going to learn the names of ten new trees and ten new wildflowers," she would have killed our enthusiasm and interest.

If you go along rattling off a bunch of names to those who are unfamiliar with them, you're going to turn them off. Have you ever attended a meeting where there were fifty or more people, all of whom were strangers to one another, and had someone suggest that each person stand up and give his or her name? After everyone had finished, could you remember their names? Bombarding kids with fifty new names while in the out-of-doors has similar results. I mentioned that names are like tools. It's the same way with a pair of binoculars, which can be used as a useful tool. But, here's how they were a dangerous weapon in my hands:

When I first began leading nature walks, I carried a pair of binoculars around my neck. It didn't take me long to discover how these discouraged various groups.

The children whom I was leading did not have binoculars. They felt that I saw things only because of this special device which they did not have. They didn't even bother to look at things they could have seen with their naked eye because they felt at such a disadvantage. It's the same way with names. If you are armed with names but others aren't, they will hesitate to participate, to discover, and to use their senses.

If I could have kept the binoculars hidden while leading various school groups, things might have worked out better. Suppose we had been looking at many sights in the forest with our naked eye before coming to an open field. Then suppose someone had spotted a large hawk soaring overhead. If I had produced a pair of binoculars at that time and permitted each child to take a good look at the hawk, the children's appreciation would have been enhanced. Unfortunately, in warm weather, I didn't wear any garments which could have kept the binoculars concealed. But if you happen to know a lot of names, you can keep these concealed; you should keep them to yourself until there is an appropriate time to mention a name.

For example, if you saw a hawk overhead and happened to know it was the red-tailed hawk, this might be an appropriate time to mention its name. If the children saw its rusty tail, you could then explain how the hawk got its name. Perhaps by knowing its name you also know something of its habits and could tell your children about the foods it eats, where it builds its nest, how high it can fly, how well it can see, the color of the eggs it lays, or any other information which might help them to appreciate the experience a little more. However, if you don't know it's a red-tailed hawk, this does not mean you cannot observe and enjoy it along with others. This does not mean you cannot compliment the child who first saw it. And if the name seems that important at such a time, give it a name or ask the kids to give it a good name.

I am asked many questions which I cannot answer, and I have never run into any real difficulty by simply telling my groups, "I don't know." Actually, the more times I make such an admission, the closer I seem to get to my group. I think they regard me as more of a human being. So I've come to the point of telling adults that the only thing they have to worry about not knowing in the out-of-doors is how to say, "I don't know." I also remind them that children aren't any more impressed by a walking encyclopedia than they are by the stationary variety that sits in libraries and many living rooms.

I wouldn't bother to discuss what one can do without knowing names if it weren't for the fact that through the years I've detected a reluctance, unwillingness, and outright fear on the part of so many adults to take children into natural areas. Several years ago, for example, I was talking to a man who explained why he didn't like taking his boy to a natural-type park. He said that no man likes bringing his boy to a place where he cannot answer the boy's questions. He said it was better for him to take his son to a baseball or football game, for he understood these sports. He added that he also could play football or baseball. Although I could not persuade this man to change his mind, I did respect him for being so direct and honest. I know there are many who share his attitudes, but there's so much that they fail to consider.

The man who takes his son to a football game can seldom answer all the questions the youngster asks. The parent doesn't know the life histories of all the players on both teams; he doesn't know all their past performance records, who they are related to, why they are playing football, the exact speed and angle of every pass thrown. But he does understand the basics of the game. He can understand and enjoy the game without having to know the names of any players on either team. He can go home and play football with his boy without having to be a professional star. He doesn't notice the questions he can't answer because he's having so much fun. He can say, "I don't know who completed the most passes last year but let's see if you can catch this long one." He might add, "That was a darn good catch," or "Nice try!" Why can't people have the same attitude towards nature?

I think much of the reluctance of adults to take kids into natural areas stems from an overemphasis on identification and scientific terminology. And the blame, regretfully, rests upon the shoulders of us who work as professional naturalists. This has not been intentional on our part but has come about because of ever-increasing demands on naturalists' time, having to keep certain groups satisfied and having to work with too large groups. This is the situation:

A group of thirty or more children, along with their teacher and several mothers, comes to a particular park to be taken on an interpretive walk by the park naturalist. Neither the teacher nor the children have ever been there. A few of the mothers might have visited the park when they were children but have been too busy to return. The adults observe, listen, and help control the youngsters as the naturalist goes into action.

The naturalist realizes this is the first time most of the children have ever been exposed to a natural environment. He also knows he will never have another opportunity to work with them and no one else will bother bringing them back. He has sixty minutes to cover what should have been covered on at least sixty different walks over a period of several years. He doesn't have time to talk about the things he doesn't know and in order to make it around the trail he doesn't have time to listen to all the questions and remarks the kids have. The teacher and the mothers go away, having witnessed a highly-regimented walk and thinking the naturalist knows everything in the fields and woods. It's something they would not care to try on their own.

Some naturalists get a kick out of impressing rather than pleasing their groups. For instance, there have been a few naturalists who have reached inside their jackets and pulled out a large snake. If a person is afraid of snakes but thinks this is what one has to do in order to lead a meaningful field trip, he'll be turned off. In recent years I've heard of naturalists eating daddy-longlegs; I guess they're supposed to taste like cinnamon. No doubt, the children would be impressed, but I bet they would go away talking more about the naturalist than about the daddy-longlegs.

People derive all types of false notions from watching a naturalist perform with various groups. Instead of watching a naturalist with a group, a person should go out into a natural area with a small group of children and observe them. See what they are interested in, be there as a coordinator to maintain order, but let the children actually do the leading. Children taught me how to be a naturalist in this very manner.

When I first began working as a naturalist, my primary interest was birds. It took about five nature walks with groups of school children to learn that birds did not interest them as much as snakes, frogs, salamanders, caterpillars, and other creatures. I knew if I wanted to have any success in working with children I would have to emphasize those forms of life which intrigued them. So we looked for frogs, caterpillars, and other forms of life and all I had to do was compliment various children for having such good eyes. I learned that children who had always been last in the classroom had an opportunity to be first in the out-of-doors. They could be the first ones to find a frog, land snail, or crawdad hole. And it was from a group of blind youngsters that I learned how hung up many of us are on having to see everything.

The blind youngsters had been "seeing" everything through the sense of touch. In one part of the forest I saw a raccoon sunning itself on a limb high above the ground. I told the group there was a raccoon above us on a limb but they wouldn't be able to see it because it was out of our reach. At that point a little blind girl turned toward me and in a cheery tone replied, "That's all right—it's nice to know that he's up there, anyway." How different an attitude from that of sighted individuals who want various animals confined in cages so they'll be certain to see them whenever they so desire.

Yes, there are numerous rewarding experiences awaiting you if you'll go into the out-of-doors repeatedly with various groups of children. Forget about the names, or, at least, use them sparingly. In the following chapter you'll see how you can be an effective interpreter of natural phenomena without having to be an expert at identification.

Some Things
To Say and Do

There are a number of activities, bits of information, and thought-provoking questions and remarks which have captured the interest of children through the years. Most of these have little or nothing to do with identification, names, or scientific terminology. In this chapter, I am sharing with you what has been of most interest to most groups. No single example, however, enjoys the same enthusiasm from all groups. So don't pick out five or six of these and think they'll work with any group of children. If your kids show little or no interest in the subject, drop it right there and go on to something else. There's plenty here to choose from, and I am confident you'll have enough things to say and do to keep any group of youngsters looking, listening, and thinking.

The interpretation of natural phenomena does not lend itself well to categorization. That's why this chapter is not divided into sections with each section restricted to trees, wildflowers, birds, etc. Things do not occur that way out in nature, and I see no sense in presenting them that way in this book.

In the out-of-doors one subject leads to another; it's difficult to restrict a walk to one subject or theme. You just have to let things happen naturally. It's the same way when I'm writing about nature. One thought or set of thoughts leads to another. Of course, there is some logic to the way various interpretive examples are arranged in this chapter.

Phenomena with similar seasonal highlights, species which share the same habitats, examples which illustrate the same types of concepts, and explanations which are part of a logical sequence of interpretive techniques are grouped together. That's the way things seem to develop when we're on the nature trail.

Subjects which have little or nothing to do with specific natural phenomena often become topics of conversation along the nature trail. Such topics are included in this chapter. Kids and adults as well seem to feel more free to reveal their thoughts and questions when they're in the out-of-doors.

Many of us have had to learn names, and it seems a shame that such learning should go to waste or be completely neglected. Therefore, interpretive information pertaining to names of common, easily-found phenomena is included. I'm not going to devote much space to telling the reader how to identify various phenomena; through modern photography and lithography we have the best field guides to identification the world has ever known. Phenomena mentioned in this chapter can easily be found in many field guides.

Some of the examples in this chapter involve broad concepts and could easily comprise the major part of an outdoor excursion. Other examples are merely remarks or questions to be used in specific situations. You will have to decide exactly how you want to use them. And don't think you have to say things the way I have said them. Be yourself in these various situations; use your own words and thoughts. I hope the following examples of down-to-earth nature interpretation will help to trigger new ideas and new thinking, bringing many new faces into the fields and woodlands.

FIRST EXPERIENCES

No matter how simple we might regard it, a first experience is a new and very important experience. Many of us lose sight of the most important aspect of a nature walk—the walk itself.

I have never been fortunate enough to see a hawk owl. If I someday see such an owl, it will be an exciting, new experience.

A child who has never walked through a woods will also find it an exciting, new experience. The most important thing is not what you say or know but what you do; your exposing a child to a new situation will long be remembered. If you remember that many children have never left the confines of various cities, any of the following activities would provide them with new experiences and are far more important than a bombardment of names and information:

1. Walking in a spring woods when buds are bursting and the air is filled with the calls of frogs and birds.
2. Walking through a woods during the summer when birds are rather quiet.
3. Walking through a woods during the autumn when all the tree leaves have colored up.
4. Walking through the woods after leaves have fallen, noticing the aromas in the air and the sound of leaves under your feet.
5. Walking in a winter woods after a snowfall has created Christmas card scenes everywhere you look.
6. Walking through a field at any season.
7. Being awake in the out-of-doors before dawn and experiencing a sunrise.
8. Sitting and relaxing on a log in the forest.
9. Watching raindrops falling on a pond.
10. Feeling snowflakes hitting one's face.
11. Walking through tall prairie grasses on a breezy summer day and watching the grasses sway back and forth.
12. Being in a woods during a rain shower and hearing raindrops hitting the foliage.

Any of these plus any of a thousand other new experiences intrigue children. Just take them for what they are. That's what I do when I see a new bird; I don't have to catch it, dissect it, and examine every cell under a microscope.

When you're in these various situations you won't have to say anything, but I bet you'll find yourself saying a lot.

WAITING FOR THAT FEELING OF CONFIDENCE

Through the years I have devoted much time to training others in the techniques of leading nature walks. Often people hesitate to lead their first walk. They say, "I just don't feel confident enough," or "I just haven't learned enough."

If people wait until they feel fully confident about their knowledge of nature, they'll probably never take that first step as a leader. The more one learns about nature, the more one realizes how much more there is to learn. All of us feel inadequate when it comes to nature knowledge.

It should be apparent that a considerable amount of nature information is missing from this book. Furthermore, more space is devoted to some subjects than to others. Do you wonder why?

I am writing about the things I do know and have experienced, and I know more about some subjects than others. If I waited until I felt well-versed on all nature subjects, this book would never be written. Therefore, if you find this book helpful, you can feel certain you can contribute something to children's lives without waiting for that day of confidence which never comes. It is like learning how to drive; you can read a hundred books on cars and driving, but you really aren't going to know what it's like until you actually get behind the steering wheel.

ENCOURAGING KIDS TO BE QUIET

Most kids become very much excited when they're in the out-of-doors for the first time. As you might expect, they do a lot of talking. This not only scares birds and other animals but it also makes talking to your group more difficult. I ask children how many eyes and ears we have. Then I ask them how many mouths we have. Finally, I ask if they think it was meant for us to talk more or to look and listen more. They usually laugh when I say, "Wouldn't we look funny with one big ear, one big eye, and two mouths?" But they get the message and begin looking and listening more carefully.

COMPLIMENTING CHILDREN

Whenever some youngster finds a bug, beetle, caterpillar, or any other creature, I take time to examine it carefully. Then I remark about its shape, color, number of legs, etc. After talking about it for a couple of minutes and ignoring the child who found it, I say, "Who found this?"

A child will raise his hand or the others will call out his name. Then I say, "Boy, it really took a good pair of eyes to see that!"

This gets the others participating, but sometimes there are some who are so starved for a little recognition they begin seeing things that aren't there—deer, fox, bears, and even elephants!

SOME KIDS ARE AFRAID OF THE WOODS

Once I was leading a group of children along the edge of a woods and couldn't help noticing that they were very jumpy. Someone would point to something and all the others would jump back. They kept asking if we were going to go into the woods but didn't seem enthusiastic when I told them we were. I asked them if they were afraid to go, and they nodded their heads. I told them there was no reason why we had to go into the woods; I suggested that we simply walk around the edge of the woods which was close to parking lots and a few buildings. This seemed to ease their fears.

While walking through a rather wet area we came upon a small patch of wild touch-me-nots. The kids were delighted with the way ripe seed pods of the touch-me-nots would explode when touched. The kids soon found and popped all of them. Then they wanted to find some more. I told them there was a large patch back in the woods. It surprised me but they wanted to go there to find more touch-me-nots. At the end of this walk I felt they had conquered their fear of the woods.

This group was from the inner city; most of them were black children. After the kids had boarded the bus, their teacher came over to me and revealed something which had never crossed my mind. She said, "One thing you have to remember, Mr. Goff, is there was a time in some parts of this country when it wasn't safe for a black person to walk through a woods." She explained that parents made up stories about dragons, large snakes, monsters, and all kinds of things, just so their children would never wander off into the woods. Some of these stories are still being told.

Therefore, it's important at the beginning of a walk to let kids know that there aren't any large snakes hiding in the trees, no lions or tigers, no monsters. I tell them the most dangerous things in our parks are bees, wasps, hornets, and yellow jackets but that these will leave us alone if we leave them alone and take a few precautions. I also caution them always to have an adult with them when visiting natural areas. If they want to know why, I tell them to ask their parents.

DEALING WITH UNRULY CHILDREN

If you work repeatedly with groups of school children, you're probably going to run into a few groups which contain unruly kids. They may crack bubble gum in your ear, scuff their feet back and forth across the trail while you're talking, and cause other disruptions. If a bus driver or extra adult is along, it's sometimes better to leave such problem children in their custody until you return from the walk with the others. Otherwise, you'll spend most of your time trying to discipline the few who aren't interested at the expense of those who are.

Once I met a group in a picnic area and was getting them together for a walk when several boys in the group began acting up. The teacher couldn't get them to behave and I was losing my patience. Finally I tore into them; the pitch went like this: "Now I can tell that some of you aren't very much interested in going on a nature walk. I have no way of knowing who can behave or who can't behave. But you know whether or not you want to go on this walk. If you don't want to go, you can stay here in the picnic area with your bus driver while the rest of us enjoy the walk; I'll think more of you and your classmates will think more of you if you'll be a little lady or gentleman—whichever might be the case—and stay behind, because if you come along and cause a lot of trouble, I'll be forced to bring the entire group back and just forget it."

Then I turned to the teacher and asked, "Don't you think that's fair enough?"

The teacher replied, "It certainly is."

We started out on the walk after all had agreed to behave. Soon the same unruly individuals began to act up. I looked at the teacher and said, "Why don't we just forget it!"

The teacher agreed and said, "This group just hasn't learned how to act."

The teacher made the entire class sit in one spot and wait until their hour was up. Then they boarded their school bus and departed.

About a week later I received letters of apology from that particular class. Each child said he was sorry for the way the "others" had acted. The following season I had a class from that same school and it was one of the best groups I ever had.

This sort of thing doesn't happen very often; during a period of twenty some years, I've had to discontinue walks for only three groups. Yes, I know the unruly kids are the ones that need the experience more than the others. But they really can't get much out of it when they're determined to be as disruptive as possible. Perhaps the greatest benefit to such children is learning for the first time that someone really means business when he/she tells them to behave.

THERE ARE NO FIRSTS

During a typical nature walk with a group of kids there often is considerable competition to see who can be at the head of the group. I like to wait until someone at the rear of the line finds a toad, beetle, or some other creature. I compliment the one who made the find and point out to the others that he or she wasn't at the front of the line. I tell the kids that in the eyes of nature no one is first unless it might be the person who sees, hears, discovers, and understands the most things.

THANKING THE TEACHER

At the conclusion of a walk, children often come forward and thank me for taking them on the walk. I like to ask them whether they can think of someone else they should thank. They are quick to point to their teacher.

Sometimes I'll have the only group in the entire park, and in such a situation I like to ask the youngsters how many other groups they have seen. I ask them where all the other children in our large city are spending their day. They tell me all of the others are probably in school. I then remind them how fortunate they are.

MY FAVORITE NATURE WALK

It is certainly impressive for a park visitor to see a dozen or more groups led by naturalists going off in different directions. But the kind of walk that impresses me most is the kind

I've been seeing more of in recent years. It's the walk in which no professional naturalists are involved; it's the family group— two parents along with two or three of their children exploring nature trails on their own. I don't know what they talk about and it doesn't matter. I do know it's the type of experience that holds families together and develops respect between the parents and their children.

PREPARING KIDS FOR NATURE WALKS

Two parents leading their own children doesn't involve all the problems one is likely to encounter when working with fifteen or twenty youngsters. Whether you're leading such a group or arranging for them to be led by another person, proper preparations can help to insure an enjoyable experience for all.

If kids are accustomed to eating lunch at 11:30, don't schedule their walk from 11:00 until 12:00. They get hungry when they're walking and can't pay much attention to anything except their stomachs.

If children are going to walk with partners, make certain all of them have partners before they arrive for the walk. If a large group is going to be divided into two smaller groups, have them divided before they arrive. Otherwise, it seems to take forever, deciding who is going to be where.

In cold weather it is imperative that boys and girls eat a good breakfast before going on a morning walk. Food in the stomach is like fuel in a stove; a little exercise through walking can generate a lot of heat. Kids should be properly clothed, too, for all kinds of weather conditions.

If you live in an area where mosquitoes are abundant, remind youngsters that they should have as much of their bodies covered as possible. Mosquitoes are a real problem to those with bare legs and arms. Even insect repellents seem to work better on clothing than on our bare skin.

If boys and girls are going to travel several miles to a park or other area, let them use the restrooms before departing. Try to arrive at least fifteen minutes before the time of your walk so they can use restrooms or get drinks of water without delaying your walk.

During the summer, kids and adults should be careful not to

use aromatic hair sprays, after-shave lotions, and perfumes. If you go outdoors smelling like a flower, the bees and other insects will treat you like one and can become real pests.

Try to train youngsters to use their eyes before going on a walk. You might place some small objects along a route and then walk the route with the kids to see how many objects they can find. You might also walk at a rapid pace with the group, and later walk at a very slow pace. They will probably find more of the objects on the second walk. This route can be along a sidewalk in the city or around a school building.

WHEN KIDS ARE LIKE ROBOTS

Sometimes teachers or leaders have frightened children into being too quiet and orderly. When the teacher introduces the naturalist and asks the children what they have to say, they simultaneously reply in a monotone, "Good morning, Mr. Smith."

The naturalist tries to get them to loosen up by asking, "Now don't you think this is a very pretty flower?"

Again, they reply in a monotone, "Yes, Mr. Smith."

The naturalist feels like a comedian who tells a hundred jokes but never draws a smile or laugh from his audience. Naturalists often discover that such groups have been told that if they made one sound, they would never go on another field trip.

NATURE REMOVES THE ROUGH EDGES

No matter what problems might be present when you begin a nature walk, the numerous encounters with natural phenomena soon cause you to forget most problems. Children soon forget their own problems associated with their homes and school. As you walk through a natural area, nature seems to slip into your group and take over. I know it's not always possible but a nature walk would be an ideal way to begin and end each day.

LIFE CYCLE OF THE FOREST

In every natural forest one can witness a cycle of life. Finding an acorn or any seed that has begun to sprout is an example of what you might wish to call the beginning of this life cycle. As you walk along or look around, point out small saplings and show how they represent another stage in the cycle—say they are like little girls and boys. Next, observe some large, mature trees and compare these to adults. Some of the mature trees might be bearing seeds; if you wish, you can say these are like people having babies. When you see a large dead tree explain how trees, like people and other living things, have a time to live and a time to die. Finally, locate a fallen log that has partially decayed and explain how it is returning to the soil to make it richer for the young saplings and fresh, sprouting seeds.

Explain that, in a sense, the tree hasn't really died but has become other forms of life. In every healthy forest there is a cycle of life which includes birth or germination of seeds, growth, maturity and reproduction, death, decay, and new life.

MOUNDS IN THE WOODS

In most wooded areas you will notice small mounds rising above the forest floor. Children often refer to these as "Indian mounds." Sometimes they ask if an animal, such as a cow or horse, has been buried in one of these mounds. Don't tell the youngsters how the mounds were formed, but suggest that by looking around in the forest they might discover clues which will unravel the mystery.

Next, try to help your children find an old fallen tree or decaying log. Ask them what they might see in its place in ten or twenty years. Someone will probably say, "I bet that's how those mounds were made!" You might add that some trees make more soil than others. The largest mounds aren't always made by the largest trees.

CRATERS ON THE FOREST FLOOR

Often, at one end of a mound you'll see a large depression in the ground. This often leads to someone's speculating that soil was dug out of the ground to bury some animal in the mound. But there's a better explanation. Again, have your children look around in the woods for clues.

Try to locate a tree which has been blown over by the wind and which has pulled its roots up out of the ground. A lot of soil often clings to these roots; where the tree had been standing, there will be a depression in the ground. After the trunk turns into soil and after the uprooted soil settles to the ground, you will find a crater at the end of a mound. Sometimes, you'll see only a crater with a deposit of soil next to it. This is the result of someone's cutting up the fallen tree, leaving only the roots and uprooted soil.

It's fun going through a large woods making note of various craters. Usually, they are at the same ends of the mounds and indicate that most trees have fallen in the same direction—away from the prevailing winds. A lot of this often occurs in the spring when there are periods of heavy rain accompanied by high winds. The soil around the roots becomes saturated with moisture and easily pulls loose from surrounding soil. The leaf-laden trees catch the wind like sails on a ship.

HOW A TREE GROWS

Most trees within a forest grow tall and straight; one sees many feet of trunk which are void of branches. Yet, higher on such a trunk, branches are quite abundant. This habit of growth has led to several misconceptions. To have some fun and to clarify how a tree really grows try this routine:

Find in the woods a small tree or sapling which still has branches close to the ground. It's helpful if you can find such a sapling next to a mature, straight-trunked tree. Point to a branch on the sapling and say, "This branch is about five feet above the ground. If this tree grows ten feet taller in the next few years, how high will this branch be if it is still alive?"

Most youngsters will reply, "Fifteen feet," assuming the branch also will have grown ten feet taller. I have a lot of fun explaining this with groups.

There might be one or two children who will maintain the branch will be only five feet above the ground. I ask them, "You mean the branch will be where it is today?" They reluctantly nod their heads in agreement. Again, I ask, "You mean to tell me if this tree grows ten feet taller this branch won't be any higher?" About the time they're ready to give in and go along with the majority in their group, I ask, "Well, just how does a tree grow, anyway?" Or, I sometimes say, "You're right! This tree could grow fifty feet taller and if this branch would still be alive it would still be right here."

If we're close to a tall mature tree, I point out how it has no lower branches. But we look up the trunk and notice the lowest branches which have died or are in the process of dying. I explain how trees have a self-pruning process whereby the lower branches and their leaves are shaded out by the higher ones and eventually die, decay, drop from the trunk, and leave scars which become covered with new bark. I point to the bark near the base of the mature tree and tell the kids that branches were growing there at one time. I ask them, "If the trunk of this tree were cut up into long boards, what would we see in the boards?" Someone will say, "Knots." I further explain that the knots represent the places where branches or limbs once grew and if the kids count the number of rings in a knot, they'll know how old the branch or limb was when it died.

To show how a tree grows in height only from the top on up, I try to find a sapling about five or six feet tall. I hold my hand about a foot from the top of the sapling after I have pulled it over and explain that the sapling might grow out as far as where I'm holding my hand, but I also point to all the branches along the trunk of the sapling and say, "But all of these will remain right where they are. They might get longer if they live and they might get larger in diameter, but their centers will remain where you see them today."

It's also helpful if you can find where a fence has been attached to a tree; you can see how the tree has grown out through the fence. Kids often laugh when I tell them that on the farm I was told not to fasten any part of a fence to a tree. Farmers at that time said the tree would cause the fence to move higher and in time all the cows would get out!

A LOG AS A RECYCLING STATION

As you examine an old dead log for mushrooms, ants, insect holes, or other signs of life, explain that many forms of life are helping the log to become soil which, in turn, will support new life. All are helpful in running this type of recycling center.

SQUEEZING DEAD WOOD

Even on some of the hottest summer days you can go to a decayed log, break loose some of the softer wood, squeeze it in your hands and watch the children's facial expressions when they see water dripping and, sometimes, running from your hands.

Compare such a log to a reservoir; i.e., a retainer of moisture for certain plants and animals which require moist habitats. Such logs make the difference between life and death for numerous plants and animals.

THE SKIN OF A TREE

Many mature trees have deeply grooved, platy, flaky, or rough bark on their trunks. But the tops of the same trees often are covered with smooth bark as are young saplings of the same species. I like to point out a good specimen to the kids and ask them which part of the tree is older—the bottom or the top?

After I am told the top is the younger portion of the tree, I explain how the bark of a tree is somewhat like a person's skin; babies have smooth, soft skin, but as a person grows older, his skin becomes rough and wrinkled.

HOLLOW TREES

Kids like hollow trees—just let them see a large tree with a hole at its base revealing a hollow interior! There will be a surge of excitement and questions will begin to fly.

Expect to be asked, "What lives in there?" You'll probably have to admit you're not really certain. I tell the children I'm not sure but it's possible that a raccoon, opossum, squirrel, or some other animal "might be inside there listening to us right now."

Sometimes we look up at the top of such a tree to see whether it is rotted away. If the upper part appears dead and contains round holes, we can surmise the trunk is hollow all the way up.

Just for the fun of it, when I'm with little kids, I like to peer into the hollow base of a tree and yell, "Is anybody home?" Quite often, some of the kids take turns at imitating my action and words.

As I slap my hand against the trunk of a hollow tree, youngsters remark about the sound. They seem to know a tree is hollow just by its hollow sound. I don't know all the reasons, but I do know that any hollow tree fascinates children more than most live, solid trees.

Children usually are surprised to learn that a hollow tree is very much alive. I tell them a tree can be completely hollowed out by decay, insects, or fire but can remain living as long as it has its "life layer" which lies just inside or under the bark. I explain that a new life layer is formed each year as the trunk increases in diameter and that this process results in the formation of annual rings which we observe on sawed-off stumps. Then I remind the youngsters that even though a large tree might be hollow and still be alive, a large solid tree can be killed if a ring only an inch or so deep is cut completely around its trunk. This, I explain, is called "girdling" a tree and is practiced by many people when they want to kill certain trees.

DEAD TREES THAT ARE UPRIGHT

Try to help others see the beauty in a standing dead tree. Often, such a tree has lost its bark and has a naked, bleached trunk. On a sunny day look for the shadows of limbs and branches against the dead, gray wood. All this silhouetted against a blue sky is a truly beautiful sight which children will long remember.

Point out the fact that a tree loses its leaves when it dies. Ask which type of tree is more likely to be blown over during a wind storm—one full of leaves or one without any leaves? Ask whether animals remain standing when they die. Get across the point that nature has intended for dead trees to remain standing for a long time. I know of some specimens which have been dead and upright for more than ten years.

Someone might ask, "But what about the trees that lose their leaves in the fall and stay that way all winter—does this help them in any way?"

To illustrate the point, ask which is broken or cracked more easily—a wet sponge that has been frozen stiff or a wet sponge at room temperature? A tree exposed to sub-zero weather has brittle wood or tissues. If such a tree also retained all its broad leaves to catch the strong winter and early spring winds, it probably would get broken off or shattered.

Now, someone might ask, "What about evergreens—don't they get more stiff in the winter, too?"

Explain how evergreens, for the most part, do not have broad leaves that catch a lot of wind, but needle-like leaves which permit the wind to pass through them more easily. Evergreens, however, do suffer from breakage during the winter—not from the wind, but from accumulations of snow and ice which build up on their boughs. Most broadleaved evergreens either grow in warmer climates or are shrubs which grow under the protection of large trees.

A TREE AS AN APARTMENT HOUSE

Whether they are dead or alive, trees with cavities or with hollow interiors house many different tenants of the woodlands. These tenants have many different appearances and habits, and they change locations from year to year. I try to reveal the entire story of such an "apartment house" in the following manner:

When a tree first begins to decay, ants and many other small insects begin eating away at the dead wood. They are the first critters to live in the tree; they make the first small apartments. Usually, the number of apartments and tenants increases.

Next, along comes a woodpecker and begins chiseling away at the tree, eating the small tenants and making a larger cavity where it and its mate will build a nest and raise their young. Sometimes it's a squirrel, mouse, or some other animal that displaces the smaller tenants. Maybe an owl will come along and displace the woodpeckers or other creatures as the cavity rots away and gets larger. Finally, when the cavity is large enough, a family of raccoons might take over. Often, raccoons, woodpeckers, insects, and many other forms of life share one tree, but each has a different place to live.

When the tree is dead, it's more likely to contain a greater number of tenants. Even after it falls to the ground, thousands of creatures live in it and under it until it has become part of the soil of the forest floor.

Remind your children how man also uses dead wood for his homes, apartments, and other buildings. We don't use green, live timbers or boards in our dwellings. Animals' needs are quite similar to our own and that's why hollow live trees, hollow dead trees, and dead logs are so important to the entire forest community.

CHANGING PLACES WITH A TREE DWELLER

After looking up into the top of a large, tall tree and spotting a hole or cavity, ask some child what it would be like to live up there. Say, "Wouldn't it be nice to be way up there and to be able to look out over the entire forest?" Get kids to use their imaginations and to tell you how things might appear if they were looking down from the top of a tree.

EXPLAINING THE LOCATION OF A TREE

I often point to a tree and ask, "Why is this tree growing here and not over there?" Someone usually suggests that a person planted the tree in its present location. I explain, through questioning and suggesting, how all trees in a natural woodland are growing where they are because of nature and not because of man. I tell the kids certain tree seeds settle in certain places because they fall there from the parent tree, are carried there by some animal, are blown there by the wind, and, in some instances, roll there because of the force of gravity. The tree sprouts and grows because the seed finds sufficient moisture, light conditions, drainage, nutrients in the soil, and other favorable conditions.

Sometimes I am asked whether a certain tree might do better if it were in a different place. I explain how the tree possibly could do better elsewhere, for example, where the soil is richer, where there is more light, or where certain other conditions are more favorable for growth. But I take advantage of such questioning and point out how a tree is not like a person—a tree accepts things for what they are. All the combined forces of nature caused the tree to grow where it is, and no matter how much better certain conditions might be in other locations, the tree does the best it can under the circumstances.

SPACING OF TREES IN A FOREST

Notice how nature has provided spaces between all the trees of the forest. They generally do not join each other side by side; they do not form walls to block vision and passage. Birds find many corridors through which they can fly, and many animals are able to see around them. Although the combined, staggered effect of many trees will block out vision from a distance, most animals can see their enemies from as far away as their enemies can see them. So, in a sense, there is a wall, but a very unique wall—one that moves back as it is approached.

Have children pretend they are forest animals, and ask how far they can see into the woods. Then walk in that direction and repeat your question. After you're well within the woods, ask your children how far they can see behind them. Then interpret one of the true wonders of the forest!

As children look around them, they'll come to realize they are within a field of limited vision. If two or three children separate themselves in a forest, each can be hidden from the others. And as they move around, the "wall" around them also will move. So, while we cannot find an actual solid wall of trees adjoining one another in the woods, we become aware of a unique woodland quality. The trees, because of their spacing, create an infinite number of walls which can exist simultaneously for animals in an infinite number of locations. This is much like trying to catch your shadow, but isn't it a wonderful phenomenon? Isn't this a pleasant change from man's building of physical and bureaucratic walls where vision, understanding, and passage often are blocked?

RECOGNIZING TREES OF THE SAME SPECIES

If you don't know how to identify certain trees, you still can determine whether two or more trees are of the same species. If their leaves, bark, buds, flowers, fruits, or seeds have the same characteristics, you can be reasonably certain all are of the same species.

It's fun to ask others whether they can find another tree like the one you're examining. See if someone can find one that's larger or smaller. If someone insists on a name and you aren't certain of the name, ask others in your party to give it what they consider an appropriate name.

COMPARING A FOREST TREE AND A TREE OF THE OPEN FIELD

Notice how trees growing out in fields and meadows have low, spreading limbs and branches. In a dense forest situation these same types of trees have long, tall trunks which are void of branches for perhaps twenty or thirty feet from the ground. Most kids have a good idea of what makes the difference. They know trees need light. Those in the forest, which are crowded by one another, have to grow tall and straight in order to receive ample sunlight. A "loner" out in a field has sunlight all around it and its growth pattern is uninhibited by others.

Every tree will take on a characteristic growth pattern or shape when given the opportunity. That's why there are arboretums around the country—they're places where trees can show off. When I feel a little philosophical, I remind youngsters it is the tree that grows alone that receives the most light—it is the one which develops to its full potential. Those growing in the forest—those which "go along with the crowd"—are affected by all the others and begin to resemble all the others, never realizing their full potential.

FINDING A PARENT TREE

Sometimes we notice many small trees which are alike; that is, they have the same kinds of leaves, bark, flowers, etc. As we search the area, we often are lucky enough to find a large tree with the same characteristics. When this happens, we can be reasonably certain we have found a parent or mother tree plus its young.

Some trees can tolerate shade and some cannot. Therefore, seeds of certain trees cannot grow in the shade of the parent tree which produced them. Out in the open, keep your eyes open for certain mature trees with a lot of young ones growing only—or at least mostly—on their south sides. Because of the more shaded north sides of such trees, their young form a semi-circular pattern on the east, west, and south sides, being most dense on the southernmost exposure.

GENERATION GAP IN THE FOREST

Occasionally, you'll come across a parent tree and its young in a woodland, and you'll notice a great difference in age between the parent tree and the others. This usually occurs with oaks and hickories.

Here, you'll notice that the parent tree might be five or six feet in diameter and may be more than a hundred feet tall. Such a tree probably would be close to two hundred years old. Yet its young might be only five or six inches in diameter, indicating they couldn't be more than thirty to fifty years of age. Surely, if the first seeds produced by the parent tree had sprouted and grown, there should be many other trees at least a hundred years old. This presents somewhat of a mystery which can be solved by looking into the history of the region or by talking to some of the old-timers still living in the area.

In many parts of our country, farmers once permitted their hogs to roam the woodlands, fattening up on acorns and hickory nuts before being butchered in the winter. The first seeds—the acorns and nuts—never had a chance to grow. Too, farmers gathered many bushels of nuts which they kept for food through the winter. And in areas where certain Indians once lived, some acorns were eaten by them, usually in the form of flour used in acorn bread. All these factors prevented the sprouting of the early seeds of many oaks and hickories. I've been told, however, that farmers' hogs played the most significant role.

After hogs were kept out of the woodlands, young saplings were able to get started. This phenomenon occurs most often in parklands in rural areas near old farms.

This explains the "generation gap" or missing generations of trees in such a situation. I really don't know how true this explanation is or how I would go about proving it, but it sounds logical and certainly would give others something to think about. If they can come up with a better explanation, so much the better!

TREE SEEDS

At any season one can find a variety of tree seeds. Not all of them will be hanging on the trees and some will be rather old and weathered. Here, it's worth pointing out that not all trees produce their seeds at the same time. Try to get a discussion started by asking a variety of questions.

Ask why not all seeds ripen at the same time. Are all seeds the same color? How do the difference in color and the ripening at different times benefit the trees and other forms of life found in the forest?

You'll find large and small seeds that are perfect spheres, seeds with wings which can twirl through the air, seeds surrounded by silky hairs for floating on a breeze, triangular seeds, and seeds contained inside fleshy and sometimes edible fruit. If we took a sack filled with a great variety of seeds and emptied it in the air about a hundred yards above an open field, would all of them end up in the same place? The seeds of some trees are designed to remain close to the parent tree that produced them, while others are designed to float for miles through the air. Those contained inside edible casings are designed to be swallowed by various creatures—rabbits, opossums, deer, birds, and others. Such seeds become exposed to the digestive juices of the animals that eat them and are scattered over a wide area in the droppings or scats of these animals. People who try to propagate various seeds find it necessary to soak them in dilute hydrochloric acid in order for the seeds to germinate. Here they are simulating the treatment the seeds would have received in some animal's digestive system. Or one might say that the tasty flesh surrounding various seeds is an enticement for animals to swallow them and thus help in their germination.

When children ask me why certain seeds have various features, I tell them this is the way they grew and since they are still around they must fit into nature's total pattern or plan. Sometimes I ask the kids, "Why do I have two ears instead of three?" Then I offer some suggestions.

For example, I explain that at one time there may have been seeds which were so conspicuous and tasty that they were chewed up and swallowed by animals and never had a chance to grow. We don't see such seeds or the trees which produced them because they're no longer around. And maybe there were some seeds contained in fleshy casings which were very bitter and, even though there were plenty of animals around, the seeds couldn't grow because they didn't get swallowed and treated with necessary digestive juices. In other words, what we see around us today are those forms of life which were able to survive because they were interrelated and lived in harmony with other forms of life.

This type of explanation usually keeps certain teachers, professors, and botanists happy, those who seem offended if you give human characteristics to plants or to other animals or who resent purposeful thinking. But when you are with children, don't be too scientific, for precise terms will hinder their enjoyment of nature. It's the same way with writing—there's a difference between readable writing and that which dwells upon precise grammar.

I bothered to include this example only because you might be with a group of children accompanied by an adult who is all hung up on the scientific approach. If you're ever in such a situation, try to compromise by taking a "middle-of-the-road" course.

At any rate, you can see how a simple topic like seeds can lead to a lot of discussion, questions, and thinking. If you listen to children's remarks about seeds and other common objects, you can be entertained for hours.

COLORS OF FRUITS, NUTS, AND SEEDS

The seeds inside many fruits are brown, and, although it would be difficult to prove, I think this gives them additional protection when they are exposed on the ground. A brown seed on the dark ground or on brown, dead leaves would be afforded extra camouflage protection. While some seeds are swallowed whole by certain animals, others are contained inside various types of casings which are not eaten by animals. These seeds either drop out of their casings or eventually become exposed as their casings decay. Such seeds would be destroyed if they were chewed up by certain animals, such as mice.

Even though some seeds are brown, the fruits which contain them are often brightly colored. The bright colors probably make the fruits more easily spotted by numerous animals. I know animals, for the most part, aren't supposed to see colors as we see them; I guess they see shades of gray. But it seems logical to assume that a bright color would be a brighter shade of gray and would still be more apparent.

Nuts and acorns, in a sense, are also seeds; at least, they are capable of sprouting. Yet those animals which feed upon walnuts, hickory nuts, acorns, and other types of nuts, destroy the meat of the nut where the energy for growth is stored. Most of these nuts remain green while they are on the trees during the summer, that is, while the leaves on the trees are green. They ripen and drop to the ground about the same time that brown leaves are appearing on the forest floor. Nature affords them camouflage protection while they are on the trees and after they have dropped to the ground. Such camouflage probably prevents all the nuts being found and hoarded by a few squirrels or other animals which happen to be first at the scene.

It is fortunate for such trees that squirrels like to bury nuts and acorns. They can't always find those they have buried and, therefore, help "plant" new trees.

Nuts and acorns have no way of getting dispersed over a wide area. They can't float on the breeze and are so heavy they usually remain where they fall unless it's on a hillside where some of them could roll to the bottom of the hill. But in time all such trees and the trees that produce them would be at the bottom of the hill. Since most of these cannot grow in the shade of the parent tree, they probably would die out. Thanks to the squirrels and chipmunks, they are carried to places where they can sprout and grow. By insuring the propagation of such trees, squirrels and chipmunks are insuring their own survival. This is but one of a thousand examples of interdependence in the world of nature.

AUTUMN COLORS

In late summer begin looking for the early signs of autumn—a red, orange, yellow, or some other brightly colored leaf. Not all the autumn colors come out at the same time. Some trees begin to color in early September, while others do not show their bright autumn colors until late October.

It's fun to play "I spy" with children. One person might say, "I spy some red leaves," and then see how many of the others can spot them. You might ask if anyone can spot any more red leaves. This works best in early autumn while most leaves are green. And it helps if you can observe a large woods from an open field about a hundred yards away. It's also fun to return to the same place week after week and watch all the autumn colors gradually come in.

If you want to tell little children that "Jack Frost" goes around painting all the leaves with pretty colors, the world won't come to an end. But there's a lot more to leaf coloration that's probably more important than frost or freezing weather. In fact, it's a very complicated process—one which I never go into very deeply because I don't have a deep understanding of it.

As the hours of daylight continue to diminish, the chlorophyll, which has been making sugars in the leaves all summer, undergoes chemical changes and loses its green color. Some sugars become trapped within the leaves and become acidic, reacting with the leaf tissue as acids react with litmus paper. And in some instances, bright pigments are present in the leaves but are hidden during the summer by the green chlorophyll. Moisture, temperature, and other factors affect the intensity and duration of various colors. A few leaves turn yellow or red in August, long before freezing weather. This early change in a few leaves often is caused by insects, disease, and injuries. We should also be mindful that not all chlorophyll is green; there is a yellowish green chlorophyll, as well as a bluish black chlorophyll. Such facts, however, don't intrigue children so much as various other ways of interpreting the phenomenon of autumn coloration.

As the fall colors begin to show more orange and red, I ask whether there's any other time that the forest might have a similar appearance. With luck, someone might suggest, "When it's on fire," or "When there's a forest fire!" Of course, trees can't think as people do, but it is somewhat of a coincidence to have this reminder from the forest at the time of year when things are usually extremely dry.

As spots of orange or red begin to appear, I tell kids these spots are like little flames or sparks in the forest. Later, leaves on poison ivy and Virginia creeper vines, which grow up the sides of trees, begin to turn orange, red, and purple and resemble flames. I tell the kids these are like streamers of flames going up the tree trunks to ignite the entire canopy of the forest.

It's also important to remind people that autumn coloration is at its best in those states east of the Mississippi River. This spectacular phenomenon is shared by only a few places in Europe and Asia. Most of the world is without it. I first became aware of this while listening to a woman from India; the woman was extremely excited over our autumn coloration and remarked that she had never seen anything like it in India or in any other countries. At the time, I thought how wonderful it would be if all countries could emphasize and be proud of their unique natural wonders instead of their military might, political systems, or monetary wealth.

SIGNIFICANCE OF BROWN LEAVES IN THE FALL

While admiring all the purple, red, orange, yellow, and other beautiful autumn leaves, I sometimes ask kids whether the leaves will keep their colors after they fall to the ground. They shake their heads and tell me the leaves will turn brown. Then I ask them whether the brown color of leaves is important to other forms of life in the forest. Sometimes someone will say they make good fertilizer and help other plants to grow. I have to agree that they do add to the richness of the soil of the forest floor, but I usually ask whether leaves couldn't make good fertilizer if they were gray or white. I tell the children I've seen sacks of gray fertilizer. Then I ask whether anything else falls from the trees during late autumn. When they mention seeds, fruits, nuts, acorns, etc., I ask what animals eat these. I hear them mention chipmunks, squirrels, mice, deer, and raccoons among others. When I ask what color most of these animals are, the children are quick to see the relationship between brown leaves and the brown animals on the forest floor. They note how this camouflage protection is provided not so much for the small seeds but for the animals which have to gather the larger nuts and acorns; it would be difficult for a hawk or other predator to pick out a chipmunk scurrying among a lot of dry, brown leaves which also might be moving about over the ground. And this protection comes when the animals need it most—right before winter when they must store away food supplies. Sometimes I ask what would happen if leaves turned white instead of brown.

IMAGINATION AND FALLING LEAVES

I like to visit a woods on an October morning, following a night of heavy frost. The slightest breeze sends leaves sailing and twirling all over the place. In such a situation, remind youngsters that the leaves have been on the trees all summer and have never been able to go anywhere. Tell them this is the only journey they ever get to make—from the tree that held them to the ground below. Tell them to use their imaginations and see if the leaves don't seem to be having a great time. Some leaves will sail about ten yards, dip toward the ground, level off, and sail on for another ten or twenty yards. Some do a rapid spin all the way to the ground—something like an ice skater's finale. There are those that go around in large circles and there are some that teeter back and forth all the way down. Some will come sailing from the woods out over an open field, traveling a distance of several hundred yards through the air. I often tell kids that it's a sign of good luck if they can catch a leaf before it hits the ground. This isn't an easy task, but kids like the challenge and take off in all directions, chasing falling leaves. Let them; let them have some fun and enjoy whatever their imaginations will bring them.

LEAF BOATS

If you're near a pond and there are dead leaves in the area, have each youngster pick out a leaf that he thinks will make a good sailboat. If the wind is blowing from west to east, go to the west side of the pond and place the leaves in the water. You can make a race out of this if you want to. The curled-up portion of the blade of the leaf acts as a sail, while its trailing stem becomes a rudder.

THE SOFTENING EFFECT OF FOLIAGE

It is a known fact that plantings of trees help to reduce noise emanating from cars, factories, and other sources of sound waves. Stand next to a woods during the winter when there are no leaves on the trees and clap your hands. Usually you'll hear a sharp echo. Go to the same spot during the summer, clap your hands as you did in winter and you'll hear no echo. The leaves absorb the sound waves.

ALL TREES HAVE FLOWERS

Every mature, healthy tree is capable of producing flowers although some authorities maintain that the cone-bearing trees do not have true flowers. I suppose I can call the latter false flowers and still consider them flowers. It's true that in some instances there are male and female trees and only the female trees bear fruits. Furthermore, the female flowers are sometimes—but not always—more conspicuous than the male flowers. There are complicated terms to describe the different flower systems which various trees contain, but I usually explain it this way:

There are male flowers which produce pollen; there are female flowers which produce the ovaries; and there are some flowers which contain both the male and female components. The latter type is referred to as a perfect flower and all trees of such a species will have these same types of perfect flowers. In some species, the male flowers and the female flowers are separate but are on the same tree. In some species, a tree will contain only male flowers or only female flowers. Pollen is transferred to the female parts or female flowers by insects, hummingbirds, and by the wind.

CATKINS

Many trees produce flowers in elongated clusters or spikes which hang down from their branches. Perhaps the best known of such trees is the pussy willow. However, if you examine a lot of different trees during the spring, you'll discover many different types of catkins. Now what does the word "catkin" mean?

You'll notice how these resemble the tails of miniature cats. At least someone once thought they had such a semblance and named them "catkins" which was derived from "kin to a cat."

LAYERS OF LEAVES

As you stand under a tree, call attention to the fact that it sheds its leaves each year. Here, of course, I'm referring to a broad-leaved or deciduous tree—one that "decides" to shed all its leaves at the same time of year. In most mature forests there are trees more than two hundred years of age. This means there are trees which have added about two hundred layers of leaves to the forest floor. As a tree grows larger, it adds more leaves each year. Ask how big a stack of leaves one might see if all the annual sheddings could be placed under a tree at one time.

A tree takes something from the soil, but it also gives something back to the soil. And the bigger it gets and the more it requires, the more it returns. What does man give back to the forest when he decides to cut down such a tree for lumber?

VARYING SHADES OF BROWN

As you walk through the woods with your group or your children, pick up a few brown leaves and notice how the brown isn't quite the same on each leaf. If you look around carefully, you can find a wide assortment of browns—everything from a light, yellowish brown to a dark, chocolate brown. It's interesting to place these side by side from the lightest shade to the darkest. This helps others to become aware that the forest floor is a blend of many shades. It also helps them to use their eyes more carefully. Some youngsters have found as many as thirty different shades of brown. Their differences are quite apparent when the youngsters hold them up, overlapping one another. However, when they throw all of them up into the air and let them return to the forest floor, the various shades are absorbed and seem to disappear as if by magic.

INTERPRETING A BURNING LOG

I often ask children whether they have ever watched a burning log in a fireplace or campfire. Most of them say they have. Then I ask them what colors they saw in the burning log. Red, orange, and yellow are the colors most frequently mentioned. Sometimes I ask, "Has anyone ever seen a green or a blue flame come out of a log?" Usually there are some who have been observant enough to have seen green, blue, and other colored flames. But they are quick to remind me that these flames never last very long.

Through discussion, children conclude that heat and light are the two main elements which man derives from fire. They also realize that sunlight is essential to the growth of trees and other plants.

Children's clothes include a variety of colors and they either tell me or I explain to them that different colors result from different types of light being reflected. Sunlight contains all the colors of the spectrum—red, orange, yellow, green, blue, indigo, and violet. I offer the following comments to think about:

A burning log was once part of a tree. It grew because the leaves of the tree received sunlight along with water and carbon dioxide for making food. This food provided the energy for growth. When a log burns, we might imagine it is giving back the light and the heat which were used in its creation. Since light contains seven basic colors, these can be seen if you carefully watch a burning log.

It's also appropriate to mention that some logs burn more slowly, give off more heat, and are considered better fuel logs than others. Oak and hickory, for example, are good fuel logs, while aspens and pines aren't so good. It seems those trees which are slow growing and have received more total sunlight are the ones which give back the most light and heat. Perhaps this is merely a coincidence but it is something to ponder.

VEINS IN LEAVES

The most conspicuous veins in leaves follow two main patterns: they either originate at one point at or near the base of the leaf, or branch out from the two opposite sides of a main vein which runs from the base to the tip of the leaf. Children might compare the first variety to a fan or spread-out tail of a peacock. The second variety might be compared to a river with tributaries flowing into it, the backbone of a fish or other animal with ribs protruding from both sides, a feather, or a tree trunk with branches growing out from two sides. Ask children to tell you what they think of when they see various types of leaf veins.

EDGES OF LEAVES

Try to find leaves that have smooth edges and some that have rough or toothed edges. Why is there this difference in leaves? I don't know and I really don't know whether anyone else knows. Maybe this difference in leaf edges is of no importance and maybe it plays an important role which no one has discovered. But it is at least important to have youngsters become aware of the fact that tree leaves have different kinds of edges or margins.

COMPARING DIFFERENT TYPES OF BARK

Mature trees exhibit a wide variety of bark patterns, and it is of interest to some groups to have these pointed out. Often one can find three trees side by side which have drastically different appearances—one might be covered with flaky bark and remind children of large, black potato chips; the second might have ridges or grooves and remind kids of a grate, register, or a folding door; and the third might be perfectly smooth and gray and make youngsters think of an elephant's skin, putty, or gray clay. Then it's a lot of fun trying to find other trees throughout the woods which have similar bark patterns. But the most fun for adults, of course, is listening to all the comparisons and remarks that come from the children.

EXAMINING A SAWED-OFF TREE STUMP

It is not difficult to find tree stumps which show the annual growth rings in a pattern of concentric circles. The distance between any two rings tells you how much the tree grew during a particular year. If you know when the tree died or was cut down, you can date each circle. Ask a child to tell you the year in which he was born and then point to the circle for that corresponding year.

Next, see if the tree has grown equally in all directions. Do the rings form perfect circles or are they a little lopsided? If the tree has grown in the open, the rings will be nearly symmetrical. Or if the tree has grown in a forest where it was shaded equally on all sides by other trees, the rings should be nearly perfect. Trees, however, don't always have such ideal growing conditions.

Trees which have grown at the edge of a woods will have grown more in the direction of a field or open area. With such a stump, simply ask why the tree grew more in a certain direction and let others come up with the reasons. While many questions can be asked and answered by looking at the growth rings in a tree stump, children usually are most fascinated by counting the number of rings and determining the age of the tree.

I have found freshly sawed-off stumps containing more than three hundred rings. To save time, I tell the kids the number of rings and ask them what this means. Most children know it means the tree was over three hundred years old when it died or was cut. Sometimes a tree with a trunk of equal size is growing nearby. If it appears to be the same kind of tree, having the same type of bark, I point to it and say, "That tree was growing right there where you see it today, long before George Washington was president of the United States. If it had eyes, ears, a memory, and could talk to us today, I know it could tell you many more interesting things than I'm going to tell you. In fact, it could probably tell us some things that would make our hair stand on end."

I also remind others how certain old trees were growing before there were any paved roads, parks, houses, cars, airplanes, rockets, radios, television sets, record players, or flashlights. Sometimes I ask children to tell me what the tree might describe to us if it could talk.

TELLING THE AGE OF A PINE TREE

You can tell the age of a pine tree without having to count the annual rings in a sawed-off stump. Pines tend to grow a new ring or circle of branches each year. If you look at pines which have grown close together, you'll notice rings of scars near the bottoms of their trunks. These rings are all that's left of branches which have long since been shaded out, died, and dropped from the trees. As you look up the trunk, these rings become more noticeable. Some will contain stubs of branches. Of course, near the tops of the trees will be rings of live branches. If you start from the bottom and count the rings all the way to the top, you can get a fairly accurate age for the tree. I say "fairly accurate" because I've been told that during years of extreme dryness or during years of unusually good growing conditions a pine might respond by not adding any new circle of branches or might end up producing two instead of one. However, I have noticed that the distance between the circles varies a great deal and assume that a greater distance means more growth. Therefore, I feel that good growing conditions put more growth on the tree before it forms a new annual circle of branches.

If you're ever in an area where pines are being cut, count the annual rings in the sawed-off trunk as well as the number of whorled branches and see whether or not they agree. So far, they have for me.

A WINTER WOODS AFTER A HEAVY SNOW

If it's ever possible, visit a woods some morning after a night of heavy snow. This is best when the snowflakes are the large, feathery flakes which cling to every branch and twig. While I've been fortunate enough to visit various woodlands following periods of heavy snowfalls, there's one such experience that I remember better than all the others. I hope you and your children someday can experience this same spectacle of nature.

It was early in November and many trees had retained their leaves, even though they had turned brown. One night it began to snow; large flakes came floating to the ground and began to build up. The city became quiet as motorists slowed down or stayed off the streets. Distant street lights were merely foggy glows in the night. Early in the morning, after more than a foot of snow had accumulated, it quit snowing. At sunrise, the sky was perfectly clear. The sun's rays were warm, and it looked as if we were going to have a nice day. I felt the urge to head out into the country to visit a large woods.

The temperature was slightly above the freezing mark and rising when I reached the woods. Already, fox and other forms of life such as rabbits, mice, birds, and squirrels had made trails and tracks through the snow. But this helped to ease my conscience; I had hesitated to spoil the beautiful white fairyland with my tracks. Everything was covered or topped with a layer of snow and was simply beautiful to look at. But other fascinating happenings soon began to occur.

Some of the snow accumulations on the uppermost limbs of the tallest trees were melting and letting go. A large clump of snow would start to fall, hit another limb which would spread it into clusters, and by the time the smaller clusters had been battered by limbs, branches, and hundreds of small twigs and stems, they became sprays of snow glistening in the sunlight and disappearing as they met the white forest floor.

Many saplings, weighed by the snow, were bent over touching the ground. It must have become colder later in the night, bringing a finer, drier type of snow, for the top layer of snow on the saplings seemed very "fine-grained." As I looked around the woods, I saw arched saplings everywhere. A few had split their trunks when they were bent over, but most of them seemed to be uninjured. Soon, snow began melting and sliding off parts of these saplings. After being relieved of a certain amount of weight, the saplings put on an unusual performance.

As snow would slide off the saplings, they would spring back into a nearly upright position, and this catapult action would send sprays of snow out into the air. This began to happen all around me and it seemed as if the saplings were doing some kind of dance. Sometimes I could see tinges of color when the sunlight struck the snow sprays. The dancing saplings plus the constant falling of snow from the larger trees created a lot of action in that particular winter woods. It also gave me a few things to think about.

If it had been extremely cold before the snow came, the trunks of the saplings probably would have become rather brittle. The accumulations of snow would have caused most of them either to split or break off. How fortunate it is for such trees that extremely cold snows are drier and finer; it seems we receive wet snows when the temperatures aren't much below freezing.

The main ingredient missing from my experience in the winter woods was a companion to share everything with. I have wondered what a group of children might have said if they had been with me. Certainly everything would have been intensified by their remarks and gestures.

Although I was alone in this particular woods, I didn't feel as much alone as I would have if I had been by myself in a large auditorium, gymnasium, football stadium, or other structure. It seems that buildings have to contain people in order to prevent a feeling of loneliness, while nature, itself, has the ability to prevent loneliness, in all its creations. It would be interesting to hear children's comments about this, especially in a quiet winter woodland.

LEAVES AND TWIGS ON SNOW

Look for places where leaves or twigs have fallen on the snow. On sunny days you'll notice how these have sunk down into the snow. Why does this happen? Why is there sometimes a crust of ice over a leaf or twig that has sunk into the snow?

Most leaves and twigs are brown, and brown absorbs more light and heat from the sun than the white snow around the leaves or twigs. As the objects become heated, they melt down into the snow. Sometimes heat waves from the objects melt the snow overhead. The resulting water freezes later at night when the temperature drops, and you see a layer of ice over the leaf or twig the following morning.

If you don't want to search for leaves or twigs, take two blocks of wood of equal size and weight—paint one black and the other one white. Place both of them on top of the snow on a sunny day and watch what happens.

FROST CRACKING IN THE WINTER WOODS

If you walk through a woods when the temperature has suddenly dipped below zero degrees Fahrenheit, you'll probably hear a new sound or series of sounds. Throughout the woods you'll hear a popping sound similar to one produced by two baseball bats or bowling pins striking each other in mid-air. This sound is caused by frost cracking in various trees.

When the temperature drops, the outermost layer of a tree trunk gets coldest. As it does, it has a tendency to shrink or contract. This shrinkage is taking place all around the tree trunk, but the inner part of the trunk is still comparatively warm and has not shrunk. Something has to give. A split suddenly occurs in the outer layer to relieve the pressure and this usually makes a loud popping sound. Some people have been able to observe as well as hear this phenomenon.

WINTER ICE STORMS

Sometimes during the winter we have freezing rains which build up layers of ice on just about everything. In our homes at night we notice the lights flickering as a result of this added weight to power lines. In the morning we have a difficult time scraping the ice off our windshields. If we turn on the defrosters to help melt the ice, the layer against our windshields melts and acts like a suction cup when we try to remove the rest which just slides around. Ice storms create many problems but they also create much beauty.

If the ice storm is followed by a sunny day with rising temperatures, try to get out to a woods and watch what happens. You'll have to be looking up into the trees and it's best if you are facing the sun.

Thin layers of ice will begin to break loose from warming limbs and come floating to the ground. They appear as light as feathers. They seem to hit the ground without making a sound, but you might detect some faint clicks as they hit other branches and break up. These thin particles of ice glimmer and sparkle as they sail through the air and provide one of winter's most beautiful displays.

THOSE LITTLE BUMPS ON LEAVES

You cannot examine many leaves on trees or on the ground without discovering various forms of bumps on the tops or bottoms of the leaves. Sometimes they are smooth and shiny; sometimes they are fuzzy; they may be smaller than a grain of rice or they can be as large as a golf ball. These are known as leaf galls and are caused by various small insects which lay their eggs in the leaf tissues. Galls are abnormal growths of cells; they are tumors caused by either the secretions from insects or the chewing action of insects.

Those leaf galls which are at least the size of a grain of corn will reveal to the naked eye the developing insect inside. With smaller galls one has to use a hand lens. After cutting myself several times with a knife, I decided it's better to open galls with the fingernails. Youngsters seem to be instinctively interested in leaf galls, especially when it is explained that the gall is the home and food supply for the "guy" living inside. I tell them that some galls remain occupied all through the winter, and I ask them to imagine what it would be like living in a big round house with plenty of food to eat all winter long, not coming outside until spring. Some think this would be great while others say they would miss the winter. But all agree how much fun it would be, staying in a large round house suspended from a tree and feeling the house sway back and forth in a breeze.

Some children seem disheartened to know we have ruined the insect's chances of developing by opening the gall. I explain it is a sacrifice and try to emphasize how the undeveloped insect will become a meal for another hungry animal. Children usually accept this as part of nature.

RELICS WITHIN TREES

There have been times when lumbermen who were cutting into trees with chain saws suddenly hit something harder than wood. Sparks would fly and the saw would jam. After removing the chain saw, they would use axes in cutting into the tree to discover the obstacle. Some interesting objects found inside such trees include flint spearheads, Indian arrowheads, or the stone head of an Indian hammer or tomahawk. Apparently these had been lodged in such trees long ago and became concealed as the trees through the years grew out around them.

I sometimes relate this information to youngsters when we are in a woods containing large trees "which were around when Indians lived here." You can do likewise and read the thoughts of children as they gaze at various trees. You might say, "I wonder what one might find if he were to cut into one of these big trees."

SLANTING TREES

Try to find a woods bordering a large open field or meadow. People often fail to notice how young trees at the edge of such a woods tend to lean or slant in the direction of the open field where there is more light.

TREES AND FUNGI

Although there are many basic physiological differences between trees and fungi, they are vital to one another in several ways. Some species of trees, for example, have difficulty absorbing certain nutrients from the forest soil without the help of fungi.

The roots of trees become smaller and smaller as we follow them through the ground; roots become rootlets and rootlets become mere strands covered with even smaller, sometimes microscopic, root hairs. The root hairs play the vital role of absorbing nutrients. But in certain species of trees, the root hairs have difficulty performing this task without the presence of the "roots" of fungi.

Fungi "roots" are extremely small and usually are referred to as "mycelia." The hair-like mycelia become intertwined with the root hairs of the tree and change certain nutrients into a form the root hairs of the tree can more easily absorb. Without this action, the tree probably could not survive. But what does the tree do for the fungus?

A fungus has no chlorophyll and cannot make its own food as green plants can. In return for its vital role in the life of the tree, various sugars made by the green leaves travel to the root hairs where they are absorbed by the mycelia of the fungus.

Now, isn't that a beautiful relationship? You won't find so many basic physiological differences between any two people in this world. Yet how often do we see so much cooperation between people? Is nature trying to tell us something?

Fungi also help dead trees decompose and form new, rich soil for new trees. The fungi receive nutrients from the dead trees and, in return, help them support new and different forms of life.

SIGNIFICANCE OF BROWN TO THE SPRING WOODLANDS

In early spring before tree buds have burst, you'll notice the forest floor is covered with brown leaves from the previous year. If you scrape away some of these leaves, you'll see many small plants which are sprouting and will soon be growing up through the leaves. On a sunny day place a thermometer under the brown leaves and note the effect they have upon the warming of the forest floor.

Do you see green katydids, green caterpillars, or other green insects? Almost all the small creatures—spiders, centipedes, millipedes, and many bugs and beetles—are brown or black. They are well camouflaged in the early spring. Most green creatures do not appear until the forest has greened up.

TREES AND SPRING WILDFLOWERS

By the first or second week in May most woodlands are full of wildflowers. The ground is covered with patches of white, blue, yellow, pink, and other brightly colored wildflowers. As you view such a scene, remind others that in June or July most of these wildflowers will be gone; they will have quit blooming and many wildflower leaves will have turned yellow or completely died and shriveled up. Why does this happen?

I ask children to name the things plants need in order to grow. They reply, "Soil, water, air, and sunlight." Then I ask which of these will not be available to the woodland wildflowers in another month or so.

Youngsters usually are quick to realize sunlight will be cut off from the forest floor when the leaves come out on the trees. I explain that by this time the wildflowers will have made food which will remain stored in their roots, bulbs, corms, etc., until the following spring when the process will be repeated. They will also have produced seeds which will become scattered over the forest.

In the woods there are some wildflowers which do not require much light. These bloom throughout the summer. There are some which keep their leaves most of the summer even though they bloom only during the spring. If a group is seriously interested in this subject, I receive a lot of questions which I cannot adequately answer.

For example, someone might ask, "If these wildflowers need sunlight so badly, why don't they grow out in the fields instead of here in the woods?" I have to admit that I don't know for certain. But I offer a few possibilities for them to ponder.

Perhaps the woodland wildflowers could not compete with the plants of the open fields; maybe the accumulation of dead leaves makes the difference. Perhaps the greatest factor is the combined effect of tree trunks, limbs, branches, and twigs.

If you watch one spot in a forest throughout a period of twenty or thirty minutes, you'll see that it alternates from sun to shade. This is merely the result of the constant change of the earth in position with the sun. All through the day, shadows of trunks, limbs, branches, and twigs pass over the forest floor. This insures light but not too much light.

But whatever the reasons may be, I know all factors are ideal for the woodland wildflowers to grow where they do; otherwise, they would be growing elsewhere. And everything must work out for their survival or perpetuation, because they return every year in the spring. They are among the many phenomena which all people can count on.

THE WITCH OF A TREE

Around Halloween it's fun for youngsters to be able to see a tree they might imagine as a witch's tree. This might be a tree with a large, strangely curved limb or simply a dead tree stub with one lone stub of a branch protruding from one side. I tell kids to imagine a witch sitting on the limb or branch beside an owl or black cat with a sliver of the moon shining behind them. Sometimes I say, "Wouldn't that make a nice picture for a Halloween card?"

NATURAL FLOWER POTS

I don't know why, but children are fascinated by hollow bowls on the sides of trees, which are produced after large limbs have died and fallen off. Soil is formed inside such bowls and plants often grow up out of them. Children call them "flower pots."

MULTIPLE-TRUNKED TREES

You might be asked why some trees in a woods have more than one trunk. I have seen trees with as many as eight separate trunks which were joined into one huge trunk about a foot above the ground. Usually, however, there are only two or three such trunks.

I try to find a stump of a tree that has been cut down within the past year or two. From the base of such a stump I'm usually able to find many new sprouts growing up around it. This helps to explain the multiple-trunked trees.

If those sprouts keep growing, they'll become trunks. And that's what has happened in the case of the other trees. Large trees at one time were cut down; the root systems had a large supply of food stored up and suddenly it had no place to go. So new sprouts erupted. Such sprouts might grow as much as ten feet in a single season.

Whenever you see a number of multiple-trunked trees, you know you are in an area where trees have been lumbered. We often refer to such an area as a "cut-over area."

WILD GRAPEVINES

We often see wild grapevines, which children call "Tarzan vines," dangling from the highest limbs of tall, straight-trunked trees. It appears the vines have grown right up through the air, attaching themselves to the limbs of the trees. However, this is not the way it actually happens.

A grapevine grows by means of tendrils which wrap themselves around twigs or limbs. As a vine grows on a small tree or shrub, its leaves, which are large, shut off the sunlight from the leaves of the host plant. As the small tree dies from lack of sunlight, the grapevine continues to grow and becomes attached to a nearby tree which is usually a little taller. This process is repeated for many years. The former host trees gradually die, decay, drop to the forest floor, and return to the soil. The vine stays up because it is firmly attached to another tree. Sometimes you can see where the vine is moving on to another tree before its present host shows any signs of dying.

Grapevines are the wanderers of the forest, creating openings which permit new species to become established. They produce fruits for many birds and other creatures. Wild grapevines are important to any natural woodland, even though naturalists often are asked, "Why don't you destroy those vines and save the trees?"

FACES ON BRANCHES

When leaves fall off tree branches in the fall, they leave scars. As a rule, trees with large leaves have large leaf scars. These resemble faces of various animals. Some look like monkeys, some resemble owls, some look like certain breeds of dogs, and you might find some which remind you of certain people. Kids have fun searching for the best ones. A hand lens or magnifying glass is helpful in this activity.

A CRASH IN THE FOREST

If you're fortunate, you might be able to hear a large tree fall to the forest floor on a quiet summer day. Rush to the spot and ask why it fell. You'll be able to see where the tree had been weakened by the workings of various insects such as carpenter ants and the growth of various types of fungi. Ask whether some insect removed the last initial support of the tree or whether a fungus dissolved just the right amount of tissue to start the mighty giant toppling. I experienced this phenomenon only once, but I still remember how everyone treated the fallen giant with respect and how a feeling of reverence prevailed as we watched its last dangling twigs and strips of bark slowly swing back and forth and finally come to rest.

LEARNING TO LIKE LICHENS

Lichens come in a wide variety of shapes or forms. Some grow as greenish gray splotches on tree trunks or upon rocks, while others grow up out of poor soils or sand in various forms, such as reindeer lichens, British soldiers, goblet lichens, and ladder lichens. But all of them have one thing in common: they are comprised of two different types of plants which live together as one.

The two plants which form a lichen are a fungus and an alga. Most fungi are commonly recognized as mushrooms, while most forms of algae are thought of as that green scum in ponds, lakes, and streams. There are also some forms of algae which grow away from water and often form a greenish cast or haze on tree trunks.

A fungus cannot manufacture its own food but has the ability to attach itself to wood or to rocks by means of acids which it produces. An alga contains chlorophyll and can manufacture its own food but has no special way of attaching itself. Somewhere along the line certain types of the two different plants became united into one form called a lichen. The fungus portion provided the "home" while the alga part made the food for itself and the "home."

Again, this is a unique example of interrelatedness in nature. And it should be emphasized whenever the opportunity presents itself.

You won't find many, if any, lichens on the trunks of trees or upon bricks and rocks within our large cities. Lichens need clean air; they cannot tolerate the fumes from internal combustion engines and other sources. When you're with a group in the out-of-doors and see lichens, tell others to take several deep breaths of fresh, relatively pure air. Lichens are living proof that the air is fit for breathing.

VARIATION IN THE THICKNESS OF BARK

It sometimes appears that large trees have had sections of their bark rubbed off or filed away. I've seen trees with several collars of thick bark separated by sections of thin bark. The best explanation I ever heard for this phenomenon was that lichens, growing on the bark, had dissolved the bark until only a thin layer remained. The thicker regions had not experienced the acid treatment of the lichens. Observing small lichens all over the thin regions leads me to accept this explanation.

BURLS

Have you ever been asked about those large bumps or swellings on the sides of trees? Often they are a foot or more in diameter. They are called burls and contain a fancy wood grain; they make beautiful salad bowls. A burl is something like a leaf gall—an abnormal growth of cells. Burls, it is believed, are caused by bacteria or viruses and possibly by the spores of fungi rather than by insects.

RAIN IN TWO FORESTS

It's a lot of fun to walk through a forest when it's raining. I'm talking about a plain shower or drizzle—not a thunderstorm. Don't ever take anyone on a walk during any type of electrical storm or when there are high winds. But when we have one of those all-day types of gentle showers, try to find a place where a deciduous forest with its broadleaved trees meets a pine forest or plantation.

As you walk through the deciduous forest, you'll hear raindrops pelting the tree leaves. But when you cross over into the pines, some member of your party will say, "Hey, it quit raining." Of course, it's still raining but the raindrops make no noise as they strike the needles of the pines. In such a situation with children, I like to walk back and forth between the two types of forest so the kids can hear the sound come and go. Few children have ever been in a woods during a shower, and they thoroughly enjoy the experience.

LISTENING TO AN APPROACHING SQUALL LINE

There are times when you'll be able to see an approaching shower. Usually you'll notice a band of gray across the sky with streaks of gray mist extending downward. This is the front line of an approaching storm. If there isn't any lightning, it's fun to stand on one side of the forest—the side away from the approaching storm—and listen to the rain coming through the trees. You can hear the rain and wind getting closer and closer until they're upon you. Then retreat to a safe place and take cover, for some electrical activity usually follows this first squall line of a storm.

IN TOUCH WITH NATURE

I have an opportunity each spring to lead groups of school kids through a beautiful arboretum which contains species of trees and shrubs from many different parts of the world. This arboretum contains a magnificent specimen of a European larch which catches the eyes of the boys and girls. I like to have them gather around the larch and examine its new spring needle-like foliage. I tell them to feel how sharp the foliage is. Of course, the green needles aren't sharp at all but soft as silk, and the boys and girls express their delight. It's at times like this that I'm overcome with a wonderful intangible or spiritual feeling.

It seems as if the children are suddenly joined or united through the arms of the majestic larch which, in turn, unites the earth and the sky. Sometimes I feel that the kids are holding hands with the earth and each other. While it's impossible for me to describe such a feeling adequately, I would like to encourage you to experience this feeling by conducting the same activity with a group of children. If you can't find a larch, try some other tree. You might want to tell the children that other children in other parts of the world might be touching the same kind of tree at that very moment. A blue sky, frogs and birds singing, butterflies going in different directions, a spring breeze, other spring sights and sounds, plus boys and girls in bright spring clothes should arouse something spiritual in even the most matter-of-fact persons.

A SONG IN THE WOODS

I had just told some third graders that everything in nature has its place when the teacher informed me they had learned a song about plants and animals helping each other. I listened while her class sang their song. Their little voices blended well with all the other spring sounds—birds, frogs, and the fluttering of leaves in the breeze.

That song couldn't have been sung in a more appropriate place. If you're with kids who have learned songs about nature, let them sing near the things included in the songs.

NATURE INCLUDES MORE THAN TREES

By now you're probably wondering why so much of this chapter has been devoted almost exclusively to trees and forests. There are many reasons, however, for emphasizing trees.

A tree remains in one place year after year; one can observe it through the seasons, watching its buds burst into leaves or flowers, observing its seeds or fruits ripening, and witnessing its change in leaf colors during the autumn. No one who wants to learn the name of a particular tree should have any difficulty doing so, for every community has a tree enthusiast, botany teacher, forester, naturalist, or the services of a university or college to assist someone interested in learning the name of a tree. If something has to be rechecked, it is easy to do so—the tree will probably still be there. This is seldom the case with birds, insects, snakes, and various other forms of animal life.

Trees and forests seem to attract people. Even park administrators when looking for parkland try to find wooded areas. I think we are so accustomed to houses and other forms of buildings that we feel more at home in a woods with the walls of trees around us and the roof of leaves and branches overhead. But don't be mistaken—a prairie, meadow, marsh, bog, swamp, desert, and many other natural areas are just as interesting as a forest.

THE MAGIC OF WATER

When you're out in the rain, skating on ice, watching snowflakes, looking at a stream or lake, hearing children remark about icicles, or watching clouds, fog, or mist, try to get others to think about the true wonders of water. Everyone knows what water is, but here we're talking about interpreting water, that is, encouraging others to have a deeper appreciation for it.

I don't know of any form of life which is not dependent upon water in some way. Most of our body is comprised of water; some animals' bodies are more than ninety percent water. Plant life, also, has a high water content. Life, as we know it, could not exist without water.

Isn't it wonderful how this compound, which we know as H_2O, can exist in three different forms: liquid, solid, or gas? The liquid form is known to most of us as rain, dew, rivers, streams, lakes, or oceans. To some children it is known only as something which comes out of a faucet. The solid form exists as ice, icicles, snow, hail, and a few other forms. The gaseous form is called vapor, steam, or humidity.

Have you ever noticed how excited a three-year-old becomes over an icicle, ice on a pond or puddle, or snowflakes? The child looks out the window in the evening and sees water dripping from the edge of a roof. Then, during the night, the temperature drops and a row of icicles is formed by morning. When the child looks out and sees icicles, he probably wonders where they came from. Did they come floating through the air and attach themselves to the roof? It's the same way with a sheet of ice on a pond—couldn't one imagine it dropped out of the sky onto the pond or floated through the air and gently settled in place?

When it is explained how water becomes ice at 32°F. or "when it gets so cold," youngsters regard this as some sort of magic. Trees are still trees, rocks are still rocks, and most other forms of nature do not change so significantly. It also is remarkable how water in a pond freezes on the top first rather than from the bottom up. If it weren't for this unique property of water, many forms of aquatic life would perish.

One of the wonders of ice is that you can skate on it, carve initials in it, chop it into pieces with an axe, or sculpture figures out of it; but when spring arrives and temperatures rise, the ice becomes water and shows no signs of having been damaged. Should it freeze again, ice will reappear but the damage won't. How wonderful it would be if other natural phenomena could erase damage with a change in temperature.

Water can create all kinds of beauty: waterfalls, sparkling dewdrops in the morning sunlight, rainbows in the sky, fluffy white clouds, snowflakes with an infinite number of patterns, babbling brooks, and blue lakes. When people decorate a shopping mall or department store with snowflakes, they use paper forms which have been cut from the same die—they all look alike. People try to duplicate nature but take the easiest route. No one has ever found two snowflakes exactly alike in nature.

Although water can create things of beauty, make life possible, and appear delicate and gentle in many of its forms, it also can be destructive and violent. The power of expansion when water changes to ice can crack the metal block of an internal combustion engine. And moisture-laden air is an essential ingredient in severe thunderstorms and tornadoes. The same substance which has caused plants and animals to live and grow can turn around and destroy them.

When we stop to consider how water can exist in three different forms—some visible, some invisible—how it can be gentle and beautiful, or violent and destructive, how it is present in all life, and how it can take life away, it is not difficult to understand why many of the major religions of the world include water in their rites, rituals, and beliefs.

IF FROGS USED LOGIC

The out-of-doors provides an excellent opportunity for emphasizing the importance of law and order. I often tell children how certain animals don't get a second chance—they're told what to do and what not to do and if they don't obey rules and laws, they don't survive. During the fall I'm usually asked what the frogs and turtles will do during the winter. I explain how these creatures spend the winter hibernating in the mud at the bottom of ponds or lakes. Then I tell the kids it's a good thing frogs and turtles don't do much thinking. Of course, the children wonder why this is so. I'm no writer of children's stories, but through the years I've developed a little fictional story which I use in such a situation.

I tell the children to imagine that the leopard frogs in the pond are like people; they can read, think, and talk. Nature has told all of them to stay at the bottom of the pond when the days get short and the air gets cold. But one leopard frog has been using a thermometer and has kept records of the various temperatures in the water. He has noted colder currents coming to the bottom of the pond while the warmer water remains on top. I call this particular frog "Freddy."

I tell the kids that Freddy Frog warns the others, "I don't think it is wise for us frogs to stay here at the bottom of the pond."

But the other frogs remind Freddy that nature has instructed them to stay at the bottom and to get ready to sleep all winter in the mud. They ask Freddy why he wants to disobey nature.

Freddy replies, "Well, fellow frogs, my records here indicate that colder water is heavier and comes down here to the bottom while the warmer water stays on top. Three days ago it was 55 degrees at the top and 50 degrees down here; two days ago it was 50 degrees at the top and 45 degrees down here; and today it is 45 degrees up there and 40 degrees down here."

Another frog asks, "What does all this mean, Freddy?"

Freddy explains, "According to what I've read, water turns to ice when it reaches 32 degrees. Therefore, it's logical to assume that we'll be frozen in ice if we stay down here. Our only hope of surviving is to go to the top of the pond where we'll be above the ice."

But all the frogs persuade Freddy to obey nature's law and he stays at the bottom of the pond watching his thermometer. Freddy is surprised, for an amazing thing happens as his thermometer readings keep dropping. Just a few degrees above the freezing point, the water begins to get lighter instead of heavier; the coldest water goes to the top of the pond, hits the freezing point, and turns to ice which helps seal out any colder air. Then Freddy and the others bury themselves under a blanket of mud and sleep through the winter.

Sometimes a youngster asks how the frogs breathe; frogs have lungs and have to surface for air during warm seasons. When they're in their state of hibernation all body processes are reduced to a bare minimum. They absorb all the oxygen they need right out of the water. Again, it's a good thing the frogs don't think about this problem.

FLOATING CHUNKS OF ICE

In the early spring try to visit a stream or river containing chunks of ice. Point out the actions of various fragments of ice. Large chunks will sail by the smaller ones; sometimes two large chunks will collide, swirl around, and then race down the stream or river. It seems they are in a big hurry even though all are destined to melt and become part of the water they are in. You, no doubt, can see an analogy between this and the rapid pace of life so many people lead.

MYSTERIOUS SOUND OF EARLY SPRING

If you are near a glen or large, rocky ravine during the first warm spell of spring you might hear a loud, explosive roar. I heard such a sound when I was a kid and it scared the living daylights out of me; I thought it was the roar of some large animal. After returning with an older friend, I discovered the source of the strange sound: large icicles breaking loose from the rocky ledges and falling on the rocks below. The rocky walls of the glen had given it a special quality. Such sounds carry a long way and you might even hear them while driving along various highways.

NATURE'S DEEP-FREEZE

When youngsters begin to ask about the value of winter, you might ask them if cold or freezing temperatures are found any-where in their homes. Someone will mention the refrigerator or deep-freeze. Get the chidren to tell you that such appliances are necessary in order to keep foods from spoiling. Explain that winter, itself, is a deep-freeze which keeps many natural foods from spoiling.

You can find fruits, such as rose hips, thorn apples, and bar-berries, which remain visible throughout the winter. Birds start moving through such areas long before new spring blossoms have produced any edible fruits or seeds. Many other animals also become more active during the first warm days of spring. Thanks to the refrigeration provided by winter, the birds and other forms of wildlife find foods that have been well preserved. And maybe some of those insects and small animals which were killed by severe autumn frosts have also been preserved and are still edible. While you're at it, remind others that bird feeders are needed as much in the early spring as they are during the winter.

THE CONSTELLATION ORION

Many planets and stars show up best on clear, crisp winter nights. One of the constellations which shows up extremely well is Orion, the Mighty Hunter. This constellation reminds me of a large kite, for part of it has a diagonal appearance. Try to locate it and interpret it for children.

You might say that many animals go into hiding when this hunter appears in the late autumn sky. They remain hidden until he leaves the night sky in early spring. Fallen leaves and snow help hide all kinds of animals while Orion is around.

PREVIEW OF SPRING

If you're in a classroom or similar situation, try to obtain a few cuttings from various trees and shrubs during the late winter or early spring. Place the stems of the cuttings in containers of water and place them in a window which receives a lot of sunlight. Then watch the buds swell and finally burst into leaves or flowers.

Don't encourage the collection of cuttings in areas where they are protected or from private properties unless you have permission. In a group of children there are usually some who come from homes where forsythias, hydrangeas, lilacs, and other shrubs grow. If each child would bring a different cutting, you could have quite a show.

It would be helpful if children could see red maple blossoms. These often go unnoticed along city streets until thousands of old ones have fallen and have given the sidewalks an appearance of being covered with bits of red sponge rubber. It would also be interesting to see a horse-chestnut, buckeye, hickory, or other large bud gradually swell and open.

Basically, this type of activity gives children something they can watch on a day-to-day basis. When spring finally arrives, they should be more aware and appreciative of certain natural events taking place around them. In a sense, you can provide such a group with two springs.

PEANUT BRITTLE ICE

Floods or periods of heavy rain followed by a sudden drop in temperature can create a type of ice which intrigues youngsters. Puddles freeze on top while the remaining water is absorbed into the ground. This results in a thin layer of ice with nothing but air underneath. Kids like to walk on this type of ice. It has a tinkling sound as it breaks; children often compare it to peanut brittle.

WINTER CREATES BRIDGES

While you are walking on frozen soil at the edge of a pond or on ice in a marshy area, remind youngsters they couldn't walk there at other seasons without getting wet feet. Freezing of soil and water makes it possible to reach new areas in winter; winter creates bridges to formerly inaccessible places.

IMAGINATION AND FALLING SNOWFLAKES

During a period of heavy snow hold your head back and look up into the falling snowflakes. If you blot out the surrounding landscape with your arms or hands, you'll experience a feeling of moving out through the snowflakes or out into space.

FEATHERS

It isn't difficult to find a few feathers while walking through the fields and woodlands. When snow is on the ground, such feathers are easily spotted. I like to find a blue, red, or yellow feather. I don't spend too much time discussing the bird that lost it, but tell everyone to look down upon the feather. Then I hold the feather up against the sky and the color disappears, becoming a dull gray. Most brightly colored feathers do not have real pigments like those in the clothes we wear. They display colors because of the way they break up and reflect light. It's simply a matter of their physical structure affecting rays of light. You can do this experiment indoors, also, by holding a feather toward a light or, in the daytime, toward a window. While this is a rather simple activity, few people, I find, have tried it.

FROZEN INSECTS

During the winter, beetles and other insects can be found under bark and logs. I've found them frozen stiff—so cold that they'd stick to my fingers. At one time I thought such insects were frozen to death but discovered they could "come back to life" after being placed inside a warm room.

Look under loose bark and logs during the winter, find a frozen beetle or ant, take it indoors and watch it "come back to life." Insects are among those creatures which spent periods of time in a frozen condition long before man considered the same practice.

ANIMAL TRACKS

If one ventures into a woods after a heavy snowfall, he realizes just how many animals live there. We seldom see a fox, weasel, raccoon, or deer; if it weren't for their tracks, we might assume they were not around. In certain parks where all animals are protected, we can point out many fox tracks. But we can also point out the tracks and trails of rabbits, mice, squirrels, pheasants, and other forms of life. The presence of these provides us with an opportunity to explain and prove how the fox does not destroy all the other animals. Of course, children are more interested in discovering more animal tracks than listening to any lengthy explanations.

I like to remind children how detectives in old movies discovered fingerprints by sprinkling a whitish powder over an object which had been touched. The powder made the print appear. I tell them nature plays detective by sprinkling the white powder all over the ground and then waiting for the prints to be made.

I once took children to an enclosure in a park where tame deer were kept. They enjoyed looking at the deer at close range. But as we continued our walk, the children were more thrilled by the tracks left by a wild deer. We tried to determine which direction the deer was traveling, whether it was walking or running, and where it stopped to chew on a branch. We did the same thing with rabbit tracks.

A set of rabbit tracks consists of two rather large tracks side by side but several inches apart and two smaller tracks somewhat staggered. We ask which direction the rabbit was traveling. Since the larger tracks obviously were made by its larger back feet, some suggest it was traveling in the direction of its front feet. This seems logical but isn't true.

When a rabbit hops, its front feet come in contact with the ground first. Then its back feet come up in front of the front feet and spring the rabbit into the air again. So the rabbit actually travels in the direction of its back feet. A few agile children usually are willing to demonstrate this unique means of locomotion.

Squirrels and certain mice move in a manner very similar to the way a rabbit moves. The squirrel's prints are closer together, however, and its front tracks are usually side by side. A mouse track, of course, is much smaller and usually shows a line in the snow where its tail was hitting.

The fox leaves a rather straight line of tracks. A set of fox tracks resembles the trail left by a large house cat. The cat, however, retracts its claws when it walks. The fox, not having retractile claws, leaves claw marks in its tracks.

As is true of other natural phenomenon, one doesn't have to be an expert at identifying animal tracks in order to enjoy them. It's still a lot of fun following animal tracks, seeing where they lead, and trying to figure out what animal made them.

MAKING RADAR EARS

When you're listening to insects singing in the fields or woodlands, frogs calling from swamps, birds calling in the distance, or any other natural sounds, cup your hands and place your thumbs and index fingers around the margin of each ear. Move your hands away from your ears and then bring them back. It's amazing how this increases the volumes of various sounds. I tell youngsters they are making ears like a deer's, and our experiment explains why deer can hear us so well. With our cupped hands in place, we swing our heads slowly from side to side and pinpoint the sources of various sounds. Children sometimes say we're a lot like radar screens.

NATURAL SNOWBALLS

A woman called me once and said she hoped I wouldn't think her question was ridiculous but wanted to know whether rabbits ever play games. I told her I had heard and read of rabbits playing in the snow on moonlit nights. She hesitated and asked if rabbits would ever make snowballs and throw them at each other. She explained further that she had seen snowballs scattered over the ground with nothing but rabbit tracks nearby. Fortunately, due to a previous experience, I was able to ease her mind.

The snowballs had been made by the wind; the rabbits had kicked up enough snow for the wind to catch and send rolling and collecting more snow. Three years earlier I had visited a large open arboretum in a park and had noticed large snowballs throughout the grounds. There were no human tracks around and my theory that kids had been rolling up large snowballs for snowmen was destroyed. We had had a heavy snowfall the previous day, followed by 50 M.P.H. winds. Once a chunk of snow began to roll along the ground the wind shoved it until its weight overpowered the wind. Some of those snowballs were more than a foot in diameter.

Another time, I saw snowballs that had rolled down a hill. I was fortunate enough to see some of these in the making—the sunlight, heating an upper ridge of exposed soil along the top of a steep hill, caused some of the warming soil to break loose, roll down the snow-covered hill and accumulate an increasing amount of snow until it reached the bottom.

Of course, if you're with kids and see any natural snowballs, it's better to ask them questions about how the snowballs were formed. Some of their ideas prove to be more interesting than the snowballs in question.

FASCINATING FROGS AND TOADS

Frogs and toads, along with certain birds, deserve some recognition as harbingers of spring. Spring would not be spring without their creaks and croaks in wooded swamps, open marshes, and other bodies of water.

Various birds return in the spring because of instinctive behavior. They often arrive while the ground is still covered with snow or while temperatures are below freezing. Frogs and toads, however, do not make an appearance until they have detected a warming trend. These critters, which have been around all through the winter, are better qualified to judge the arrival of spring than some "fly by nights" arriving from regions a thousand miles away. When the temperature is suitable for arousing these amphibians from their winter's hibernation, it's a sure sign that tiny rootlets have begun to inch through the soil and that bulbs and seeds have begun to sprout. When that first frog bursts forth with a song, we know wildflowers are pushing up through the forest floor and many forms of life have begun to stir.

The first frog to sing in the region where I live is the wood frog which measures a little less than three inches in length. It is best identified by its black robber's mask. This frog often appears before the ice has completely melted from woodland waters. Its call is a coarse clacking, resembling the quack of a duck; a group of wood frogs singing resembles the quacks of a flock of startled ducks. This amphibian has the distinction of being found farther north than any other amphibian or reptile in North America. It is found in Labrador and Alaska!

When the first warm rains arrive, our fields and woodlands are filled with the calls of spring peepers and chorus frogs. Children mistake them for the sounds produced by crickets and other insects. Spring peepers prefer brushy, second growth areas while the chorus frogs choose more open areas. Even so, their habitats overlap considerably.

The spring peeper's scientific name is *Hyla crucifer. Crucifer* refers to the X on its back which resembles a cross if one can stretch his imagination. The peeper's call is a high, piping whistle—a single clear note repeated about every second. People can imitate its call and induce it to answer. Many are surprised when they discover that such a loud note comes from a frog scarcely an inch long.

The chorus frog is found in a wide variety of places and is common in the city wherever water accumulates in ditches or vacant lots. Its call is a vibrant "crreeek," resembling the sound produced by one's running his thumbnail over the large teeth of a metal pocket comb. This frog usually has three imperfect stripes down its back. It's about the same size as the spring peeper.

After the peepers and chorus frogs have begun to sing in great numbers, one might hear a deep, rattling snore interspersed with clucking grunts. This is the call of the leopard frog which gets its name from the roundish black spots on its green back and legs. Remind youngsters that this frog has been invaluable as a laboratory animal; some of us would not be alive if it weren't for research which utilized the leopard frog.

As the spring warming trend continues, gray treefrogs begin to sing. They emit a soft, low-pitched "cherrr." The gray treefrog has a mottled appearance and can change color; it might be gray, brown, green, or almost white. It is the best camouflaged frog of our region and is usually undetected when perched on a lichen-covered tree trunk or limb.

In late April or early May the night air is filled with a long, musical trill. Such a trill might last for thirty seconds. If you listen carefully you'll hear considerable variations in these calls.

First, a low-pitched trill begins. Soon it is joined by a high-pitched trill. Then, more and more calls of varying pitches and rates join in the chorus, creating one of the most beautiful blendings of sounds in nature. These calls are produced by American toads. An American toad can sing thirty vibrations per second! On a night when a storm is approaching, the calls of American toads have a special quality—something like the effect a rainy day has upon the sound of a train.

The American toad often is confused with Fowler's toad. Experts maintain that the two species hybridize; consequently, identification is difficult. Generally, the American toad has one or two warts on each of the raised splotches on its back while Fowler's toad has three to five such warts. However, there's nothing confusing about their calls; Fowler's toad sounds like a little lost lamb. It emits a short, nasal, and unmusical "w-a-a-a-a-h!"

After the permanent bodies of water have warmed, one hears an explosive "ka-tung!" It sounds like a loose banjo string and is produced by the green frog. This frog is about three and one half inches long and is best identified by folds of skin extending back along its sides. The bullfrog, with which it is confused, has no lateral folds extending the length of its body trunk.

Bullfrogs usually begin to sing in May. The call of the bullfrog is a series of vibrant, nasal bass notes. It reminds me of a cow bellowing. I have yet to hear one say "jug-o-rum" in spite of this popular description.

About the last frogs to sing in the spring are the little cricket frogs which are about the same size as spring peepers. As one drives along the highways with his windows down, he hears their calls coming from small streams and ponds. The call can be simulated by striking two hard pebbles together. It is described as "gick, gick, gick" or "Click, clack, clickety, clack, clack, clack." Sometimes, what seems like a bunch of cricket frogs singing, turns out to be just one little frog.

These are the frogs and toads that I know best; there are many others that are not mentioned. All are interesting and worthy of one's recognition. And kids love frogs and toads. Just tell them you're going to try to catch a frog and place some emphasis on "catch." Then watch the fun. I let the kids catch a few frogs each spring. The group usually decides that the frogs should be released. This is somewhat of a gimmick but I don't think it hurts the frogs or anything else.

FROG HABITATS

There are reasons why some frogs are found in ditches or temporary pools of water while others are usually found in permanent bodies of water. The primary reason for frogs and toads singing is to attract mates. Masses of eggs are laid in the water not long after these amphibians begin singing. It takes varying lengths of time for the hatching tadpoles to develop legs which will enable them to travel on land. Those that develop their legs in one season usually can be ready to leave the water temporarily; that is, until they can find another body of water. Spring peepers and chorus frogs are examples of frogs whose tadpoles develop in a relatively short time. Even so, during dry springs they become trapped in receding waters and are easy prey for predators.

Bullfrogs and green frogs have tadpoles which do not develop all four legs until their second year. This is why they are found in permanent bodies of water.

SALAMANDERS

About all I ever do with salamanders is look for them while I'm with the kids. The most common form in my area is the redbacked salamander. This species lives under old logs in the woods. Kids enjoy turning over logs in search of these fascinating tailed amphibians. I let children handle them if they first moisten their hands by squeezing some water out of the dead log. Sometimes there's a puddle nearby and it suffices. And we always question the kids until they agree that the logs should be placed back in their original positions.

Here we are trying to teach the children to have respect for the salamander's rights—rights to a home and freedom. We are careful not to put the salamander where the log might crush it; we place the log in position and then release the salamander next to it. This helps teach a reverence for life. I can't prove it but I believe these values go far beyond the salamanders.

WATER STRIDERS AND SURFACE TENSION

Anyone who has spent much time around a pond or quiet pool of a stream probably has seen water striders or skippers scooting about over the surface. Some call these insects "water spiders," but this isn't a good term because spiders aren't insects. And if you examine a water strider closely, you'll discover it has six legs instead of a spider's eight. However, a spider chased from its hiding place along a bank can run over the water without breaking through the surface tension.

Surface tension is another unique physical property of water, and water striders help illustrate how it works. On a sunny day when you can see the shadows of water striders on the bottom of a pool, you'll notice circles around the shadows of their feet. These circles show how the surface of the water has been pressed down by their feet—you're really seeing the shadows of circular depressions in the surface of the water. I tell kids it's a lot like bouncing your fingers on top of a bowl of gelatin; if you don't press too hard, you can make a depression without breaking through. A needle can be made to float on top of a glass of water by this same principle. Place the needle on a piece of soft tissue paper and gently lay the tissue and the needle on the water. As the tissue becomes saturated, gently press around its edges until the tissue sinks; the needle will stay afloat if you don't bump the glass or the table.

I tell children the top layer of water is stronger than the rest of the water. Many animals depend upon this strength referred to as surface tension.

FOOLING A WATER STRIDER

After explaining to children that water striders eat many other aquatic insects as well as small insects which fall on top of the water, I tell the kids if they can find some small seeds we can have some fun with the water striders. Of course, during their search for tiny seeds they encounter many natural phenomena. Sometimes the kids become so interested in other types of life that I have to find the seeds.

I take one seed at a time and throw it onto the water within a foot or so of a water strider. As the concentric rings or ripples from the splashing seed reach the water strider, it traces them to their source and pounces upon the seed. Soon, realizing it was fooled, the water strider lets go of the seed and resumes its search for real insects. We don't always succeed in fooling the water strider; at such a time I tell the youngsters "he" probably wasn't hungry. If you don't want to search for seeds, carry a few light seeds in your pocket; rice would be the right size but it sinks too fast.

LIGHT UNDERNEATH AND DARK ABOVE

Water striders, small fish, tadpoles, and many other forms of aquatic life are light on their undersides and dark on their backs. A predator in the water, looking up at them from underneath, has difficulty seeing them because their light undersides blend in so well with the light sky. A predator looking down on them from the air has difficulty seeing them because their dark backs blend so well with the dark bottoms of the pools or streams.

A CLICKING IN THE PINES

Early one spring after we had had a few warm, sunny days, a friend called me and said she had been standing by a pine tree and had heard a clicking sound. She asked if the pine cones could be making such a noise. I told her I had never heard of such a thing—and I hadn't. She brought me a few pine cones several days later and told me to take them home and watch them.

After the cones had been on my table for several hours, I detected a faint click. Soon there were other louder clicks. During the night all the pine cones opened up. When the compartments in a pine cone open, they do so with a click; at least, this has been true for the red and the Scotch pines.

If you're near a pine tree whose cones are still closed and it is a sunny day, listen for a clicking. Or take a few tightly closed cones inside and listen for the action.

SPRING SNOW

It's fun to get out after a heavy spring snowfall, especially if the sun is shining. Notice the bases of trees, shrubs, and weed stalks. You'll see where the snow has melted back from them, creating many craters in the snow. The dark trunks or stalks absorb a lot of sunlight and as they heat up, they melt away the snow. This also happens in the dead of winter, but it is much more apparent and happens more quickly in the spring when the sun's rays are stronger. Yes, nature has utilized solar collectors for a long time.

DANDELIONS

Everyone knows the dandelion, but there might be some information pertaining to the dandelion which people are not aware of or haven't bothered to think about. When children are asked how the dandelion got its name, they often reply, "Because it's dandy like a lion," or "The yellow flower looks like a lion's mane."

I tell them the name does have something to do with a lion. Then I pick one of the dandelion's leaves, hold it up sideways, and tell the kids to look at the sharp points along the edge. I ask, "What part of a lion do those sharp points make you think of?"

Youngsters are quick to see the resemblance to teeth. I tell them that's what a Frenchman thought when he called it, "dent de lion," which means "tooth of the lion." With older students or adults, I ask if anyone can speak French. If someone volunteers, I ask him to say "tooth of the lion" in French.

After picking the stalk and yellow flower cluster, I hold them up and ask, "How many dandelion flowers have I picked?" Most youngsters will say I picked only one flower. Then I pick the cluster apart and hold up one of the many small flowers which grow together in one cluster. I explain that many flowers are composed of small blossoms growing together and are commonly referred to by botanists as "composites." Sunflowers, daisies, zinnias, asters, and marigolds are examples.

THE CIRCLE CONCEPT

There are numerous geometric designs in nature, but it becomes apparent after observing a variety of natural phenomena that the circle or sphere is the most common and important. Here are a few examples of circular or spherical patterns in nature:

1. Holes in the ground made by crawdads, chipmunks, ground squirrels, woodchucks, and other animals.
2. Holes in trees, made by woodpeckers, sapsuckers, insects and other animals.
3. Annual growth rings in stumps.
4. Round trunks of trees.
5. Cross sections of most plant stems.

6. Certain spider webs.
7. Numerous wild and domestic flowers.
8. Certain mushrooms.
9. Raindrops and hailstones.
10. Grapes, oranges, apples, and other fruits.
11. Galls made by insects on various plants.
12. The sun and the moon.
13. A halo around the sun or the moon.
14. Concentric rings of ripples produced when an object drops into a pond.
15. Many animal eggs and plant seeds.

We find a few plants with triangular and square stems; we find examples of pentagons, hexagons, and other geometric designs. In fact, we have been able to find every type of design people have made. But the circle is predominant. Perhaps you are wondering why I'm making such a fuss over something so obvious. I do so because this illustrates one of the few lessons the human race has learned from nature.

I often ask children if we'll see triangles, squares, or circles if I throw a round stone or mudball into the pond. Of course, they know they'll see concentric circles. Then I ask, "But what will we see if I throw something square or triangular into the water?" Seldom can I fool them; they know even a square or triangular object will produce circular ripples. After we have looked around and discussed all the circular designs, I suggest, "That circle is a mighty important design to nature. Do you think it is important to us?"

Sometimes I ask how the earth travels around the sun—in a triangular, square, or circular path. I remind youngsters this orbit probably existed before man appeared on this earth. Before I let the kids tell me about all the ways we use the circle, I give them something to think about.

In the early history of man, when he had something heavy to move, he would get about a hundred other men to help him. They would shove and pull the heavy object over the ground, straining every muscle in their bodies. Yet all around them nature was displaying the importance of the circle. It was as though nature were a voice saying, "Look, man, the circle—that's the important design. Why don't you pay attention? Why don't you use this design?"

Finally, probably by accident, man discovered an object being shoved over a log rolled and moved more easily. In time, this discovery led to the wheel and to all the other circular designs so important to all of us.

Children begin listing all types of circular designs which include buttons, watches, clocks, gears, plates, cups, glasses, door knobs, phonograph records, telephone dials, and flying saucers! Here we are on a planet that travels in a circular orbit; the fact that we are interrelated with everything else on this planet is reinforced by the circle's being most common and important to all. I prompt kids to think further by saying, "I wonder how many other lessons nature is trying to teach us today."

THOUGHTS IN A MEADOW

I like to look out over a large field or meadow and point out patches of different kinds of plants. Some are tall while others are short; some bloom every year while others require a second year of growth before blooming; they are of many different colors; they serve many different purposes; and they have unique qualities. But they live together, side by side, and no single species takes over the entire meadow. Here we see complexity, but we also see harmony.

CAMOUFLAGE GAME

Give children crayons, water colors, or any other coloring devices and a supply of paper, cardboard, illustration board, or similar material. The material should be cut into a variety of shapes—circles, squares, elongated rectangles, triangles. Encourage the youngsters to color a variety of designs and patterns—spirals, dots, and anything else their imaginations may create. The cutouts should also contain solid colors; that is, some should be solid white, black, and brown. Some should be large while others should be quite small. After each child has made about a dozen cutouts, divide the children into two groups and lead them along a trail, preferably one going through a woods as well as through heavier undergrowth.

Pick out a spot and instruct one group to place their cutouts in various places where they'll be camouflaged. Every cutout has to be visible from the trail and at least half of it has to be exposed.

Next, take the second group to another location along the trail and have them follow the same rules. After everyone has carefully placed all his/her cutouts, let the two groups exchange places and see which group spots the greater number of camouflaged cutouts.

There are a few tricks to this game, and children need to be given ideas on how to fool the human eye. They can thus be introduced to the principle of "deceptive camouflage."

A large white cutout might be placed on a black or brown tree trunk while a small black or brown cutout also is placed on the same tree. The eye is attracted to the more conspicuous white form and often overlooks the one which is well camouflaged. Cottontail rabbits and certain birds with white outer tail feathers use this principle in fooling their enemies. When a cottontail suddenly changes direction or when the birds land and fold up their white feathers, their pursuers, who have had their eyes fixed on the white parts, completely lose sight of their potential prey.

All groups have had fun with this camouflage game. Adults seem to enjoy it as much as the children.

GRASSHOPPER'S DISAPPEARING ACT

Along a dusty lane and in sandy areas, we often see a large grasshopper take off from the ground. While in flight, it displays yellow underwings which catch our eyes. When it lands, the underwings are folded under its brownish forewings and we lose sight of it. A bird chasing such a grasshopper also is fooled and will sail right over the spot where the grasshopper has blended in so well with its background. Let children have fun trying to catch one of these grasshoppers and point out how difficult it is to see one which has landed.

EARTHWORMS

Remind others when they have found an earthworm or fishing worm that some authorities maintain if we had to pick out one creature which is more important to our survival than any other, it would probably be the earthworm. Soils could support little, if any, plant life without the workings of earthworms.

Earthworms keep the soil turned and fresh by continually bringing older soil to the surface. Their tunnels permit air and water to circulate better throughout the soil, and many of their activities help to recycle many forms of organic materials. Life, as we know it, could not continue without earthworms.

So don't write the earthworm off as a "nobody." Kids are fascinated to know that in some countries certain species of earthworms attain a length of six or seven feet! And as is true with all forms of life, the earthworm is interrelated with other animals—birds, such as robins, woodcocks, and a few others, survive by eating large numbers of earthworms.

Many children do not understand why there are so many earthworms out on the sidewalks, trails, and pavements following a heavy rain. Be sure they understand these creatures have been flooded out of their homes and have not come out in order to get in the water.

BEES AND OTHER POLLINATING INSECTS

You cannot observe many flowers without seeing bees and other insects. In order for plants to be healthy through the years—that is, from one generation to the next—pollen must be transferred from one flower to another. I simplify matters by telling children if it weren't for the bees and a lot of other insects, we wouldn't have watermelons, tomatoes, peaches, pears, apples, strawberries, and many other fruits unless each of us spent most of our time with a little brush going from one flower to another. Just think of all the work and time these insects save us!

SPIDERS

If I had to pick one group of phenomena which have provided the most hours of enjoyment in the out-of-doors, it would be the spiders. And the champion of these is the little crab spider, a creature about the size of a pea. The body is shaped like a crab and the spider holds its legs in a crab-like manner. This little spider can also walk sideways like a land crab. I find crab spiders during the warmer seasons by shaking the plants out in the fields or at the edges of woods. As I run my hand up the stalk of a plant and give it a few shakes, the crab spider suddenly appears, dangling from a silken thread attached to the plant.

I reach out and grab the thread, breaking it loose from the plant. Then the spider comes up the thread to my hand. After

I show it to all the kids, I bump one hand with the other and the spider again descends on its silken web, which is shot out from one of the spinnerets at the tail end of its body.

Sometimes the spider comes back up the web to my hand. I shake it down again, and it comes back up. Kids observe, "It's a yo-yo spider." If it's a clear day with a gentle breeze and blue sky, I move out into an open area with the spider. I tell the kids to stand far back, give the spider a lot of room and he'll do a trick for us.

I bump my hand, the spider drops down on the sticky web attached to my hand and hangs suspended in the air with its body perpendicular to the ground; that is, its head is facing the ground. Soon, however, the spider assumes a horizontal position with two or more of its legs on each side held closely together extending straight out from its body. In this position it appears to have wings. Kids sometimes say it looks like an airplane. When the spider gets in this position, I know it's getting ready for further action.

Next, two or more glistening strands of web go shooting out into the breeze—sometimes these are twenty or thirty feet long. As the breeze lifts these strands into the air, the spider releases its hold on the web going to my hand and begins floating on the other strands. As soon as it gains an altitude of about five feet, I tell the kids to hurry in under it, point to it and keep watching it. They see the spider go higher and higher into the sky on its silky strands of web. Often, after the spider is out of sight, we see the strands glistening as they are struck by rays of sunlight. Then the children scramble for another crab spider.

The youngsters know what to anticipate when they find another crab spider. I don't know why but they usually want to give me the spider instead of trying the trick for themselves; maybe they realize how much fun I'm having and simply want to help. With the second act I try to throw in a little drama or humor. As the spider descends from my hand on its silken strand I say, "All systems are go and we are continuing countdown!" When the spider shoots other strands out into the air, I say, "We have ignition!" Finally, when the spider lets go and begins floating on its longer strands I exclaim, "We have liftoff and all systems are looking good!"

The kids usually laugh at my remarks and often throw in a few of their own. Youngsters often have yelled, "Up, up, and away!" If the spider, while ascending, happens to be approaching a tree, we wonder if it will clear the obstacle. When it goes over the tree, there's a spontaneous burst of applause from the children.

Sometimes a crab spider will float along on its web only two or three feet above the ground. If the children close in too quickly, they shut off the breeze. I have to tell them to back up and give it more air. We have had crab spiders travel about thirty yards, remaining only a few feet above the ground. Suddenly, a stronger breeze catches the web and the spider takes off in a steep climb. At times the web hits a shrub or tree and the spider climbs up the web and scurries under a twig or leaf. Once crab spiders light on a shrub or on the ground, they perform like real escape artists. They get under a blade of grass, leaf, or twig and are difficult to find.

This process, whereby spiders travel through the air, is referred to as ballooning, and I tell the children that spiders were the world's first balloonists. Children are amazed to learn how spiders can travel several hundred miles in this manner and go as high as airplanes. I also explain that inside the spider's body the web is a liquid much like water; the split second it meets or mixes with air it solidifies and becomes web. The organs for producing web are called spinnerets and are situated at the tail end of the spider. Some spinnerets can make a sticky web and some can make a dry web. The instant a spider is shaken loose from an object it shoots out a sticky web which hits and sticks to the object, thus preventing the spider from falling too hard or too far.

Most small spiders are able to balloon, and nearly all baby spiders travel in this manner when they first emerge from their eggs. We have noted, however, that it is difficult to get a spider to balloon on a day when the sky is overcast or when there is an approaching shower or thunderstorm. The spider either drops all the way to the ground or travels a few feet through the air and descends to the ground. I like to find the fluffy, parachute-like seed of a dandelion or milkweed and release it in the air. If it takes off and goes up into the sky. I remark to the boys and girls, "This is a good day for spiders." Of course, my remark draws either a frown or a whimsical expression from the teachers accompanying the children.

Children rarely show any fear of the crab spider or any other small spiders. Unless I'm asked, I don't say anything about dangerous or poisonous spiders until after the "performance." Then I explain that even though I have never been bitten by a spider, many people say they have suffered from numerous spider bits. Occasionally, while a small spider is walking around on my hand, a child will ask if I'm afraid of it. One might ask, "Won't that spider bite you?"

I reply, "Why would the spider want to bite me? I'm not squeezing or hurting it in any way and spiders eat insects—not people."

I tell the kids that as far as I know, all spiders can bite if they want to and all of them are poisonous; that is, all have some poison which is used for paralyzing their prey. Of course, the black widow and brown recluse spiders can be deadly if they happen to bite someone, and they should never be handled. Fortunately, these deadly spiders are not found on the plant stalks and shrubs of the fields and woodlands. I also point out that I do not pick up the spider between my thumb and index finger. Instead, I chase the spider with one hand onto my other hand. Then I interchange hands so the spider can keep walking around.

It's rather difficult to get a spider to walk on your hand. Often, with large spiders, I simply keep placing my hand in front of them so the children can see the spiders keep changing directions, avoiding my hand. This provides substantial evidence that spiders have no desire to get on people.

Don't make too big a deal about handling spiders. If you prefer, you can get a spider on a stick, piece of cardboard, glove, or any other object in order to make it perform. I sometimes do this when I detect too much interest in my not being afraid of spiders. We want children to talk about the wonders of a spider and not about "the guy who's not afraid of spiders."

With larger spiders, which get shaken loose from branches, I grab the web and hold the dangling spider near a shrub or tree. Soon it shoots out a sticky web which hits and sticks to a branch. The kids' eyes nearly pop out of their heads as they watch the spider walk right through the air to the point of attachment. If they're in the proper position, they can see the web. During this performance, the spider depends upon the web sticking to my hand as well as the one sticking to the shrub or tree. And I have to keep my hand in one place until the spider is "home free." Children often refer to such a spider as a "tightrope walker."

It's also a lot of fun observing spiders at night. Hold the back of a flashlight against your nose and look down the beam as it slowly scans some grass or leaves. You'll see some bright dots of light, something like dewdrops with a bluish green glow. These are spider eyes. Slowly walk closer and closer to the shining objects and you'll be able to spot the spider. We have spotted spider eyes from a distance of about thirty yards, closed in on the spot, and discovered to our surprise a spider no larger than a grain of corn. This is a good time to tell others that most spiders have eight eyes—some are for daytime vision while others are for nighttime vision.

You can have fun looking for spider eyes at night in your yard or in your home if you happen to share it with spiders. Once I placed a spider in a closet during the day and had several others take turns looking at its eyes with a small flashlight.

During the fall we see the large circular webs of spiders which are commonly referred to as orb weavers. A series of spokes or rays extend out through a spiral pattern of rings. Such a web provides a good opportunity to examine two different types of web. If you touch the spokes or rays, you'll discover they are strong and tend to bounce off your finger as you tap against them. But when you touch the circular part of the web, it sticks to your fingers. This is a good time to mention that spider silk is the strongest natural fiber known. It is still a mystery how a spider can walk over the sticky part of its web without getting stuck. At night it's fun to hold a flashlight beneath such a web so that the web splits the beam from the flashlight. This helps to show off the beauty of the web, and various colors sometimes appear, glistening in the light. If dewdrops are on the web, it's even more beautiful.

If you find a large circular web during the day and see a large black, white, and yellow spider perched in the middle of the web, you can entertain children. Simply touch the spider with your finger and it will start bouncing back and forth against the web. The entire web will begin to shake back and forth. Why the spider does this I don't know. I do know that kids usually liken this performance to that of an acrobat on a trampoline.

Can a spider do a free fall; that is, can a spider ballooning at a high altitude let go of its web and fall several thousand feet before shooting out a streamer of web, enabling it to make a soft landing? Do spiders really do this? Once I was asked these questions by a "slow learner," and I've been wondering about them for a long time.

Another delightful aspect of spiders is that they haven't been made so much a subject of naming. Even to adults a spider is simply a spider and they can enjoy it for what it is without having a label get in the way.

FILMY DOME SPIDER

In shrubs or small trees look for a spider web that looks like an inverted bowl suspended between two networks of strands. This web shows up best on a foggy morning or when there is a heavy dew. The network of strands above this bowl puts on a spectacular display when it is struck by rays of sunlight, especially when a slight breeze causes the strands to move about. As you look into the upper network, you'll see needles of light shooting in all directions. I know of no other web that has this special quality; it seems to belong exclusively to the filmy dome spider, one of the few spiders I know by name.

One morning during a dense fog I drove to a park where I was to meet and train a group of volunteer naturalists. As we walked a woodland trail, we were thrilled by filmy dome webs all about us. Some of the domes were nearly a foot in diameter while others were only three or four inches across. It seemed that every shrub contained three or four of these. We walked on to an open area but returned along the same trail about an hour later, after the sun had warmed things up. Although we were on the same trail, we could not spot the domes of this spider; they had disappeared as if by magic. Sure, the webs were still there—they just weren't visible without the heavy dew.

SUGARING FOR MOTHS

Various sweet concoctions can be prepared and smeared on tree trunks during the summer and fall to attract moths and other insects. This can be done in your own yard, a camping area, or in a public park, provided you have permission to be there after dark.

I mash up a few bananas, brown sugar, either a bottle of stale beer or a package of dry yeast mixed with white sugar and warm water, and enough corn syrup to make the mixture thick and sticky. About an hour before sunset, I go along a trail and smear the sweet concoction on various tree trunks. A whisk broom has worked better than any other device for this task. A watery solution will work but presents a problem on warm nights—the solution evaporates in a hurry and if it is smeared on dead trees or dry bark, it is immediately absorbed. So try to prepare a thick solution.

After dark go out with flashlights and observe all the beautiful moths and other insects feeding on your baited trees. If you look down a beam of light at a moth's head, you'll see its eyes shining a beautiful orange or pink. If you are careful and don't wave your flashlights all over the place, the moths will usually remain feeding while a light is on them. Many people have never seen a moth with its "tongue" uncoiled, dabbing about in its food supply. You'll find many other insects, such as ants, beetles, bugs, and wood roaches. Explain that insects can detect aromas from a great distance—certain moths can detect an odor over a mile away!

KIDS AND CATERPILLARS

The young of many animals are simply miniature forms of the adults. The young of insects, however, seldom resemble their adult parents. The young of many insects are called larvae, and perhaps the most striking of all larvae are those of moths and butterflies. Such larvae are called caterpillars. It is believed that the word *caterpillar* was derived from the Old French *chatepelose* which meant "hairy cat." Many caterpillars are quite fuzzy and children seem to take to them as they would to little kittens.

Kids often want to keep caterpillars and say they'll feed them lettuce at home. That's when you should say, "Let us permit the caterpillar to stay where we found it, for it probably feeds on only two or three kinds of leaves."

It strikes youngsters as a miracle the way such worm-like, crawling creatures can become transformed into beautiful, delicate, winged moths and butterflies. Tell them the caterpillars would not become such beautiful creatures if they didn't eat the proper foods. Remind them that children, too, must eat proper foods if they are to grow up to be healthy adults. Milk to a baby is like sassafras leaves to a spicebush swallowtail caterpillar. You might even use a few comparisons to persuade boys and girls to eat spinach and other green vegetables.

TENT CATERPILLARS

Soon after the leaves have unfolded on wild cherries, little splotches of silk begin to appear in the crotches of the limbs or branches of the trees. The splotches grow until they are about six inches across; they are made by larvae known as tent caterpillars. Their silken tent can repel rain like a tent and it somewhat resembles a tent. Children are fascinated by such a structure.

We look out on the limbs near the tents and usually find the cluster of eggs which the young hatched out of. This cluster resembles a spot of burnt sugar or syrup, the kind made in the oven when a fruit pie boils over. The young tent caterpillars are especially beautiful when viewed through a hand lens; they are blue, yellow, gray, black, and a little orange or yellow. They attain a length of about three inches and can be found wandering around on limbs where they spin a silken trail. Finally, they find a hiding place on the ground or in a crack in the bark and spin cocoons. Later in the summer the newly hatched adults mate and eggs are laid on another branch of wild cherry where they will spend the winter.

Most children aren't too much interested in the life history of tent caterpillars; they are captivated by the tent and the fact that they can handle the caterpillars. Sometimes a child will say, "Look, he likes me."

WOOLLY BEARS

On chilly autumn mornings look for woolly bear caterpillars on fallen leaves. These caterpillars are black at both ends and rusty brown in the middle. Some people believe a lot of black foretells a severe winter; some even go so far as to say that more black at the front means the first part of winter will be more severe.

The woolly bear caterpillar hibernates through the winter. The following spring it spins a cocoon on the ground and later emerges as an adult Isabella tiger moth, a handsome creature. But kids show more interest in the caterpillar which, like the children, is also immature. Although the caterpillars are curled up on a cold morning, the warmth from children's hands soon has them crawling about. And boys and girls love this display of friendship.

CLICK BEETLES

Click beetles can be found on tree trunks, under the bark of dead logs, and on leaves of various plants. The one most commonly encountered is rusty brown and about an inch long. Most adults have seen click beetles many times, but children seeing one for the first time are thrilled.

The click beetle gets its name from the way it clicks and throws itself into a somersault after being placed on its back. When held between the thumb and index finger this beetle will often click repeatedly. Hold one near a child's ear so he can hear how sharply it can click.

Place a click beetle on its back on a billfold, piece of cardboard, or any other flat surface. In a few seconds the beetle will click and spring about six inches into the air. If it lands on its back, it will repeat this performance until it lands upright. Sometimes the click beetle opens its outer hard wings and takes off flying with its more delicate wings which have been concealed. This is a revelation to many children who don't realize that hard-shelled beetles which usually crawl around have the capability of flight.

If you examine the underside of a click beetle, you will notice a little point or projection extending from the back of its body into a little depression in the middle of its body; there's one of these on each side. When placed on its back, the click beetle arches its back to raise the projections out of their sockets. When the beetle suddenly straightens out, the projections fall into their sockets with such force that it causes the hard wings to bounce and send the beetle tumbling through the air.

TRAPPERS IN THE SAND

Perfect funnels in sandy, shaded areas reveal we have discovered the homes of ant lions. These insect larvae remain buried in the sand at the bases of their excavations and wait patiently for an ant or other small insect to topple in. If the victim begins to climb to the rim, the ant lion throws sand and causes it to fall back to the bottom. If the ant lion is hungry, it grabs the victim in its mandibles, pulls it under the sand, and enjoys a good meal.

You can tickle the sand inside the funnel with a blade of grass and get the ant lion to respond. When I was a kid, I knew the ant lion as a doodlebug. I was taught to place my mouth near the funnel and say, "Doodlebug, doodlebug; come up, come up." The ant lion would sometimes begin to move and I was certain it had understood my words. Probably vibrations from sound waves or air currents caused it to react.

I seldom find ant lions in open sand dunes. Instead, they seem to prefer shaded areas under or near trees where the sand is more gray from organic matter. This gives them perfect camouflage. It is sometimes difficult to locate that first funnel. But once you discover one, you'll notice many more; it's simply a matter of knowing exactly what you're searching for.

Scrape away the sand and uncover an ant lion so children can see it. Place it on your hand and have the youngsters observe how it moves backwards. Kids are sometimes afraid of this ferocious-looking critter but soon lose their fear as they watch its antics. After everyone gets a good look, place the ant lion on some loose sand. It should begin backing down into the sand. I usually say, "There he goes; he's going, going, going — ." The kids interrupt with "Gone!"

The ant lion is the larva of a winged insect which resembles a small, slender dragonfly. This is a rare case where the adult is named for the larva; the adult is known only as an adult ant lion. This larva is quite clever, being able to spin a silken cocoon under the sand without getting a grain of sand inside the cocoon.

STARS IN THE SAND

If you're in a sandy area on a dry day, look for whitish, shriveled-up mushrooms which resemble ping-pong balls which have been crushed by heavy feet. During a heavy rain these same mushrooms take on a different appearance—they open up, appear fleshy, and have tentacle-like projections surrounding a puffball. The puffball has a hole in the top and if you tap on the ball little puffs of "smoke" come out of the hole.

This type of mushroom is called an earth star or geaster. Geaster is derived from "geo" for earth and "aster" for a star. A dried geaster can be placed in water and will open up within five or ten minutes. Removed from water, it slowly dries out and shrivels up into its original position. I've had an earth star for five years and it still opens when placed in water!

By opening only during a rain, the earth star insures its propagation. Drops of rain hitting its puffball force little clouds of spores out of the hole. Since everything is wet, the spores stick to the sand. If all conditions for growth are met, new earth stars will begin to grow.

MIGRATORY BIRDS

The appearance of spring birds in regions which experience severe winters is always a pleasing sight. When you are with others and see some of these birds, explain the true significance of the birds' actions. Some birds return to our regions to nest while others simply pass through on their way to points north.

In early spring the insects begin to stir. If unchecked their numbers would become staggering. Fields and forests would be stripped of vegetation, many forms of animal life would be infested with parasites, diseases spread by some insects would be rampant, and all of us would run the risk of being destroyed.

Ducks and geese are among the earliest arrivals to attack various insects; warming waters contain many larval and nymphal stages. Insects invading the shores and those out in the fields and meadows are attacked by squadrons of sandpipers, plovers, and other shore birds. Insects in the forests are attacked by wrens, thrushes, sparrows, and other birds later in the spring. Some insects that try to fly away are picked out of the air by flycatchers.

By May many insects have managed to hide under leaves, in bark crevices, and on the undersides of limbs and branches. And there are thousands of insect egg clusters getting ready to hatch and produce millions of insects. Then, waves of warblers and vireos move through the trees, picking off eggs, larvae, nymphs, and adult insects. They are like little vacuum cleaners and cover every branch, bark crevice, and leaf.

I once heard a man say that if all the birds in the world quit eating for two full days, the human race would probably be destroyed by insects. I'm not sure we'd be destroyed but I am sure, from watching spring birds, that we would have many severe problems if it weren't for their work which many of us never notice.

WHY THE BIRDS DON'T DESTROY ALL THE INSECTS

While giving the preceding interpretation of bird migration you might be asked whether the birds destroy all the insects. You know they don't and there are good reasons why some insects survive.

Insects are needed for the pollination of flowers which become the fruits and seeds eaten by many animals, including people. Many insects are required as food by resident birds and other forms of life, such as snakes, frogs, toads, lizards, salamanders, and fish. Insects also play vital roles in the overall life of the forest; for example, they and their larvae help logs and dead trees decompose. Perhaps one of the most obvious advantages of birds leaving some insects is so the insects will multiply and be a ready source of food for them when they pass through our regions again. And we have to remember that among the insect survivors are included those insects which help to control others. Yes, nature in its infinite wisdom protects and provides for all.

BIRDS AND FOOTBALL PLAYERS

Look at the plates in any good book on birds and you'll notice that many birds have black over their eyes, under their eyes, or through their eyes. The northern yellowthroat is one of many which have a perfect black mask. Even the bright red male cardinal has a black splotch around its eyes.

Certain football players smear a black concoction under their eyes on bright, sunny days. This helps to reduce glare and enables them to keep an eye on the football. It is also possible that the black around the eyes of birds helps them see insects or potential enemies much better.

MIGRATING BIRDS AT NIGHT

During the spring and autumn bird migrations it is possible to hear birds overhead at night. I first experienced this while walking through a large shopping mall parking lot near my residence. They produced the best effects on nights when there were low, misty clouds. I heard chirps, tweets, and all kinds of notes just a few feet above my head, but I was never able to spot any of the birds. I was told that the lights in the parking lot might have had something to do with the birds passing over. You can hear better if you cup your hands by your ears and hold your head straight back. See if you don't get the feeling of hearing little ships signaling to each other on a foggy ocean.

HORNETS

Those large, gray, somewhat cone-shaped papery nests that we see in shrubs or trees during the summer, fall, or winter are made by the bald-faced or white-faced hornets. The occupants aren't interested in people unless someone is foolish enough to disturb them. Hornets have an interesting life history.

A lone queen begins the colony in the spring. The newly hatched eggs are infertile females and are known as workers. They help the queen build and enlarge a new papery nest. Hornets chew up old wood into a paste; when the paste is spread out into a thin layer, it dries and becomes paper. Hornets and other paper wasps were probably the world's first paper makers.

The hornets work all summer, making the nest larger and larger to accommodate the growing population. In the fall a new fertilized queen leaves the nest to hibernate through the winter. All the workers and males die and the nest is never used again by any hornets. This is similar to the way people build all types of structures which eventually are evacuated and become ruined.

I have found queen hornets hibernating under logs. The queen excavates a depression in the ground and also chews out a hollow cap directly above the depression. This makes a comfortable little room in which to sleep the winter away.

Another naturalist once told me that he could handle the queen hornet without getting stung. One rather warm day in late November, I found a queen and picked her up in my hand. The children accompanying me watched as the hornet began walking around. I noticed the tail end of her abdomen moving up and down, and when she found the most tender part of my finger, she let me have it. The kids burst forth with laughter as I suddenly dropped the queen. But it really didn't sting too much; I thought the queen was maybe giving me a "gentle" warning.

In winter it's safe to examine the hornets' nest. Young "detectives" will notice different colors in the paper. Explain that the different colors came from different colors of wood which the hornets changed into paper.

YELLOW JACKETS

Yellow jackets are social paper wasps that prefer to build their nests underground. They occasionally build in other places, such as under the eaves of buildings, under old siding, and in attics. Yellow jackets resemble honeybees but have brighter yellow on their bodies. Honeybees usually are busy traveling in rather straight lines between their hives and sources of nectar or pollen, whereas yellow jackets tend to pester people by hovering around picnic tables and other sources of meat and sweet concoctions. They get on my nerves but have never stung me; I have felt their wings touch my ear as they flew about my head.

I have to agree with those who point to bumblebees and call them yellow jackets; the bumblebee does appear to be wearing a fuzzy yellow jacket or sweater while the yellow jacket doesn't. I don't know who gave all the creatures their names, but I try to go along with the majority to avoid further confusion.

Yellow jackets catch and chew up many insects which they feed to their larvae inside their papery nests. So they are beneficial in helping to control other insects. However, they do present a problem if a group ever steps on one of their underground nests. They immediately pour out of the ground and attack every member of the party.

In summer and fall it's a good idea to walk on hard trampled trails or paths; yellow jackets prefer to build their nests under softer soil. If you wander from an established trail, you run a greater risk of disturbing yellow jackets. And this applies to woods as well as open fields.

INSECT SOCIETIES

Hornets and yellow jackets along with honeybees, ants, termites, and certain other insects live in highly structured societies. One might wish to call them political systems. There are similarities and differences among all of them. In spite of differences, one does not try to destroy or change all the others. Hornets live in their nests in trees, honeybees live inside trees or manufactured hives, yellow jackets may be underground, ants live in a variety of ways in the soil or in dead wood, and other social insects live in various similar ways as they have done for thousands of years. They all seem content to live and to let live. Maybe people, regardless of religious beliefs, political systems, and so forth, should be more like the social insects, living in a variety of ways without interfering with the lives of others.

LINES OF ANTS

Did you ever watch a line of ants going back and forth over a sidewalk, picnic table, or tree trunk? If you did, you probably noticed how two ants going in opposite directions seem to bump heads, hesitate, and then continue around each other. Such ants find their way by the sense of smell and not by sight. They follow the trail by smelling it, and they can tell by smell whether that other ant is one of their own kind. When a gap occurs between the ants, take your finger and rub it back and forth across their trail. You're rubbing away the scent the ants have been following. Then watch the next ant when it comes to the rubbed-out section.

The ant will suddenly stop, turn from one side to the other, backtrack, turn completely around and appear startled. Finally, after wandering around, it will pick up the trail again and things will return to normal. Kids get a big kick out of this activity. Some sugar or a piece of fruit placed on a sidewalk will usually attract ants and get a trail system established.

WHY INSECTS SING IN LATE SUMMER

Katydids, tree crickets, and certain other insects do not begin their singing until summer or fall. We notice their chorus by late summer. Children wonder why. The answer is simple—these insects grow in stages, shedding their skins several times before they are fully developed. Until their wings are sufficiently long or properly developed, they cannot use them for producing their characteristic sounds.

RACES WITH BEETLES, BUGS, AND OTHER CRITTERS

Kids can catch or capture certain insects, which do more walking or running than flying, and have fun entering them in races. Draw a small circle with a diameter of about a foot. Beyond the small circle, draw a larger one the center of which is the same as that of the smaller one. With a stick I simply make a circular line in the sand or soil. Then each child takes one critter and when I give the signal drops or releases the "racer" inside the smaller circle. The first bug, beetle, daddy long-legs, or other subject to cross the larger circle is the winner. You'll be surprised how excited the children will become over this activity, and you just have to disregard the expressions of other curious adults who go away scratching their heads. Any harmless creature can be used for this activity. We reward the winner by permitting it to be the first one returned to the wild.

CHIPMUNK'S LUNCH COUNTER

On stumps and logs you will often find the remains of acorns, seeds, and nuts which have been eaten by chipmunks or similar animals. Tell the kids this is the chipmunk's lunch counter or dinner table and that he is a rather sloppy housekeeper.

SIMULATING FOSSILS

Small children occasionally have difficulty understanding or appreciating how fossils were formed. You can help them gain a better understanding by mixing plaster of Paris with water until you have a thick paste and pouring part of it into a box, milk carton, or can. Pour in about two inches of the paste and then place several pieces of seashell macaroni on or in the mixture; pour in another inch or so and keep repeating this process. When the plaster of Paris hardens, remove it from its mold and tell the children it's a man-made rock. Break it open at various places and let the children see the seashell impressions or fossils. In nature, live animals with hard shells were the macaroni, while sand, clay, and other materials in water formed the plaster of Paris.

A STAKE AND ITS SHADOW

When you begin a walk or activity on a clear, sunny day, take time to drive a stake into the ground and place a small twig at the end of its shadow. Tell the boys and girls you'll return to the spot in about an hour, at the end of the walk. Ask them if the shadow will be in the same place. Will it move to the left or to the right? Will it be longer or shorter? Don't give them any answers; they can see who is right when they return to the spot. If clouds should in the meantime blot out the sun, tell the kids to try the experiment on their own at the same time of day in their own yards. This gives youngsters a greater awareness of the earth's changing position with the sun.

NATURE'S BADGES

You can seldom walk through the summer or fall fields without picking up all kinds of sticky seeds on your clothes. Such seeds often are referred to as hitchhikers. When the kids ask me about them, I tell them to think of such seeds as badges—instead of nature's giving us a merit badge, gold star, or achievement award, she gives us seeds. These seeds prove we have spent time in the out-of-doors. After such an explanation, I stick three or four different types on my shirt pocket or coat, stick out my chest and say, "See, these prove I've been exposed to nature." On many occasions, after making such a remark, I've had my clothes picked clean of seeds by children who hadn't "received their share." A boy told me in a letter how much he enjoyed the "badges." At the end of his letter he wrote, "By the time we finished the walk I was a 51 star general."

MUDBALLS AND CRAWDAD HOLES

Near the banks of streams as well as out in open fields you'll find round holes made by crayfish or crawdads. I say "crawdad" because children seem more intrigued by this informal term. Some holes will have a mud chimney around them, while others will simply be holes in the ground. I roll up a ball of mud and tell the kids to listen very carefully when I drop it into the hole; I tell them they might be able to hear it splash in the water way down under the ground. Incidentally, this is about the only time I can get a large group of children to be perfectly quiet! I drop the mudball, there's a slight pause and then a splash or "kerplunk," followed by the children's cheers.

SOUNDS OF THE SEASONS

Regardless of the season, try to pay attention to its characteristic sounds. Nuts falling during autumn, frogs calling in the spring, howling wind and slapping of bare branches during the winter, and the soft quietness of summer are but a few examples. If recordings were made in the out-of-doors at various seasons, a person sensitive to the sounds of nature could listen to the recordings at any season and tell when they were made.

WET HANDS FOR MOIST CREATURES

Kids often want to hold salamanders, small frogs, and other amphibians which normally have moist skin. If such animals are held very long in a dry human hand, the animals will die. But as long as the kids keep their hands wet by repeatedly dipping them in water, they can handle amphibians without harming them. If an animal is moist or slimy, one should have moist hands when he holds it—that's a pretty good rule of thumb!

WHAT IS A MUSHROOM?

To most people, mushrooms are round, fleshy objects on the tops of fleshy stalks growing out of the ground. Some make a distinction between mushrooms and toadstools, assuming that mushrooms are edible while toadstools are poisonous. Most people know that mushrooms and toadstools are types of fungi.

Actually, the term "mushroom" may be aplied to mushrooms, toadstools, puffballs, coral fungus, and many other forms of fungi. The mushroom is simply the fruiting or reproductive body of a fungus; it is the part which produces spores. Spores are somewhat analogous to seeds; they are capable of germinating and growing new fungi if they find proper conditions.

The vegetative or non-fruiting portions of most fungi are hidden under the ground or within decomposing logs and stumps. Molds and mildews also are forms of fungi but do not produce large, easily-observed spore-producing structures. Athlete's foot is a type of fungus which lives on human beings.

To children I explain that the large, visible forms of fungi are somewhat like apples or flowers on apple trees which have their trunks, branches, and roots hidden, showing only their flowers and stems or their fruits and stems.

Picking a mushroom does not destroy the fungus any more than picking an apple would destroy the apple tree. However, in public parks and other places such picking does cheat some-one else out of having a chance to discover something beautiful.

A FAIRY RING OF MUSHROOMS

Out in open fields during the fall you should be able to find colonies of mushrooms growing in nearly perfect circles. These have been referred to as "fairy rings" because it was once "be-lieved" that fairies came out of the woods and danced around in a circle thus creating the ring, and, incidentally, making a nice story for children.

When a spore of a mushroom settles in a place where it can grow, vegetative parts extend or grow out in all directions from the spore. At the ends of these vegetative parts the fruiting bodies or mushrooms appear above the ground at certain seasons. Since the growth is uniform, the mushrooms form a circular pattern. At other times you might notice rings of dark green grass among the lighter grass. The mushrooms will appear here, and the grass is healthier because the "roots" of the mushrooms help make nutrients more readily available to the grass roots.

I have also noticed that the most nearly perfect circles of mush-rooms occur in the open fields, especially in pastures. Fairy rings occur in wooded areas but they are seldom circular. Why the difference? Out in the fields the soil and plant life are more uniform, allowing all parts to grow at the same rate. In a wooded area the vegetative parts of the fungus would encounter various obstacles such as tree roots, tubers of wildflowers, and different types of soil conditions. Therefore, in the woods they grow in irregular loops instead of perfect circles.

HOW ONE STOMACH CAN ROB THOUSANDS OF MINDS

One autumn I was able to show thousands of school children an old white oak stump which was covered with beautiful orange and yellow mushrooms. The children were thinking of Halloween, and the orange and yellow mushrooms reminded them of candy corn. I told one group this particular kind of mushroom was good to eat and was known as the beefsteak mushroom. As soon as I had finished my remarks, a little girl piped up, "They're good to look at, too." Her innocent but meaningful remark gave me a lot to think about, especially the following autumn when I anticipated showing the same phenomenon to other school groups.

The mushroom appeared again the following autumn and looked more dense and succulent. I had many school groups scheduled to go on walks and was looking foward to sharing this beautiful phenomenon with them. But when I approached the old oak stump with a group of children one morning, I could tell something was wrong. When we were upon the site, we saw that all the mushrooms were gone; all that remained were the flat, whitish stubs where they had been cut off with a knife. Yes, someone knew they were good to eat and had taken them. He/she didn't mean to cheat thousands of school children out of seeing something for the first time. The person just didn't stop to think how removing something from nature can feed one person's stomach, while leaving it in nature can feed thousands of hungry eyes and minds.

NATURAL AREAS PROVIDE MENTAL NOURISHMENT

It's a good gimmick and most people are intrigued to know that certain wild plants are edible. But there just aren't enough edible plants in most protected natural areas to feed all who visit them. One specimen of an edible plant can feed only one person, for example. But this same specimen can be examined by thousands of people if it is not destroyed. This is somewhat of a paradox, for there is a value in experiencing a new taste in a plant grown by nature. We have to decide what is best for all concerned, and I'm not sure I know.

With most groups I try to take a middle-of-the-road course, explaining that there is a difference in someone's tasting a blackberry for the first time and someone's picking a bushel of blackberries in order to "live off the land," which, in many instances, is either another person's land or land which is supposed to belong to everyone. We have transformed many natural areas into agricultural lands so we could grow fruits, vegetables, and other food products. The few remaining natural areas have to provide essential intangibles which food products do not provide.

You may or may not agree with this concept. However, if you bring up this subject when you're with a group, I think you will agree it's a good conversation piece.

Even if you know a certain mushroom or fruit is edible, be careful about telling this to children. Later they might see what appears to be the same but isn't—the results could be tragic. Tell them not to eat any fruit or mushroom unless it has been positively identified by an expert.

AND I DON'T WANT TO KNOW

Anyone who tries to learn the names of plants and animals soon discovers it's impossible to learn all of them in a lifetime. I'm thankful I don't know the name of every natural phenomenon. Mushrooms, for example, represent a group of plants I've placed in my own private category of phenomena whose names I don't try to learn. Of course, I can't help picking up a few names from various mushroom enthusiasts.

When I look at most mushrooms, I usually see them for what they are; I can enjoy and appreciate their colors and shapes without any names or labels crossing my mind or getting in the way. I might view ten different mushrooms of the same species but see each one as an individual.

What would it be like if every person were known as either John or Jane Doe? I'd rather know them as individuals without knowing their names. One precise term or name for thousands or millions of representatives of one species takes something away from each one's individuality.

Sure, names have their place and you can have a lot of fun learning to identify plants and animals if you so desire. But not knowing certain names can be fun, too. There's ample opportunity for both.

WORKING WITH THE BLIND

Don't ever pass up an opportunity to take a group of blind children or adults on a nature walk. You'll discover this can be one of the most rewarding experiences of your life. Again, however, it isn't so much a case of your doing something for others as it is permitting others to do something for you.

I've led many groups of blind children and adults on nature walks and feel disgusted when I hear about special trails being prepared for the blind where they can follow a rope and read signs printed in Braille. Why does this have to be? Sighted individuals either transport or lead the blind to such trails. Why can't these same individuals take them on a walk as they would any other group? Nature has its own "Braille" in the edges of leaves, patterns and textures of bark, fuzzy and smooth leaves, soft moss, and a myriad of other textures, shapes, and patterns. In addition, the blind will help you become aware of sounds previously ignored, aromas in the air, and many other rewarding revelations.

WATCHING WATER DROPLETS

Did you ever watch a droplet of water fall from a high ledge all the way to the ground? It's difficult to see the globular shapes of raindrops as they go falling past our field of vision. But we can see the beauty in a water droplet if we use the right technique.

Find a place where there is a slow but steady falling of droplets. Then throw your head back and look at their point of origin. When you see a droplet begin to fall, keep your eyes focused on it and bring your head forward and down, following the droplet all the way to the ground. This is the only way I've been able to witness the beauty in such a droplet. Simply watching one fall to the ground gives it the appearance of a streak, and it's difficult to follow one with your eyes unless you move your head right along with it. This can be done in the cities where droplets fall from high buildings.

POWER OF A HAWK'S EYE

I've heard various tales about a hawk's power of vision. Some of these were probably exaggerations, but I think it would be safe for you to tell children that most hawks, if they knew how to read, could read the headlines on a newspaper more than a hundred yards away. Remind others how a hawk, which appears no larger than a twenty-five cent piece way up in the sky, can spot a mouse running in the weeds or grass on the ground.

FIREFLIES

Most children are acquainted with the insects known as fireflies or lightning bugs. Actually, if we want to be correct, we should remember these insects are neither flies nor bugs. Instead, they are soft-shelled beetles. This seldom is of much interest to children, however. They are more interested in the little creatures for what they are. This insect's remarkable light, known as a "cold light," triggered off a lot of research. This research led scientists to developing fluorescent lights.

GLOWWORMS

Throughout the summer and well into autumn one can observe glowworms in moist areas in and around most woodlands. If you're near a small stream at night, for example, have everyone turn off their flashlights and watch the ground or muddy banks. Soon you'll see a little green dot begin to glow and slowly become brighter. This is the glowworm. Pick it up and you'll see it looks more like a bug than a worm. Then turn out your lights again and keep watching.

Often you'll see hundreds of little greenish lights appear along the banks or upon the moist ground. These are truly beautiful in the darkness of the woodland night. Kids sometimes say they are like neon signs in the city. It is not unusual to hear an adult in the group say he had often sung a song about a glowworm but "this is the first time I ever saw a real one."

Explain that the term "glowworm" refers to both the larva and the wingless female of the firefly or lightning bug.

FANTASTIC PHOSPHORESCENT PHENOMENON

I've never seen anyone who didn't become excited when we discovered greenish, glowing logs during night hikes. Such wood resembles radium and is referred to as "fox fire." Fox fire is probably a mispronunciation of the term *phosphor*. Due to the presence of the mycelia or vegetative portions of certain fungi within the wood, chemical changes occur which produce phosphors. Phosphors in such wood oxidize very slowly, giving off a steady glow. This is similar to the "cold light" of the firefly, but the firefly regulates its glow by controlling the flow of oxygen to the lighted part of its body.

You won't find fox fire every night you walk in a woods. It seems at its best after periods of heavy rains during the summer and early fall. I found it in the same woods for three successive years the first week of August. The fourth summer was extremely dry, and I could not find any fox fire. Fox fire is worth searching for—it's one of those things people never forget.

VALUE OF PREDATORS

From time to time I'm asked whether weasels, foxes, wolves, hawks, owls, and certain other creatures which have been singled out as predators are of any value. Such a question reveals that the person is not aware of the valuable roles of the predators. I explain that predators help to control population explosions in nature, that they prevent the rapid spread of disease by eliminating animals which are diseased and weakened or not so alert, and that they prevent prolonged suffering in sick or injured animals by quickly putting them out of their misery.

Why certain animals have been called predators is a mystery to me. The dictionary defines "predator" as an animal which habitually preys upon other animals. A robin, then, would be a predator because it preys upon earthworms; a fish would be a predator because it eats aquatic insects; and man would have to include himself in this category unless he were a vegetarian. Somewhere along the way, probably through the efforts of game biologists and sportsmen, an animal was considered a predator if it preyed upon those animals which man also wanted to hunt or eat.

Most good sportsmen realize how predators help to improve and safeguard various game species. I tell children that animals can't go to a supermarket and buy so many pounds of mice, rabbits, or frogs. They have to do their own hunting and "butchering" if they are going to have meat "on their tables." Those that aren't successful starve to death. Always stress the fact that one animal is getting a meal. Is it better for an animal to slowly starve to death or be killed unexpectedly?

WHAT GOOD ARE MOSQUITOES?

Few people have any love for the mosquito and often ask whether such a nuisance is good for anything. I explain that mosquito larvae are an important food item for other species of aquatic life. Certain birds and a few other creatures also consume many adult mosquitoes. And it's possible this insect might have a value not yet discovered by man. If I'm in a cantankerous mood, I sometimes ask, "What good are people? What have we, as a group or species of animal life, done to make this earth a better place for all types of life to live? Have we made it better for ourselves?"

CLOVER LEAVES

Lawns and fields usually contain some variety of clover, and children have always felt fortunate if they could find a clover leaf with four or five leaflets. Few have carefully observed the clover leaf at night, however.

On a summer night when dew is forming on blades of grass, take a close look at clover leaves. Notice how each leaflet closes along its middle vein and how all three leaflets come together.

TWINING OF VINES

Vines often grow in a spiral around the stems of wildflowers and small trees. Most people have observed them. Ask how most of them grow; that is, do they grow clockwise or counterclockwise? The vast majority of those I've observed were growing counterclockwise. I've been told that in the lands south of the equator vines tend to grow clockwise.

THE QUIET EXPERIENCE

Take time to sit down with your children near a babbling brook, quiet lake, open field, or within a dense forest. Simply have them remain absolutely quiet for five or ten minutes—tell them to listen, to relax, and to think. This type of quiet experience has always been rewarding.

WHO USES THE LAND?

Naturalists who work for public agencies responsible for acquiring and preserving natural areas often encounter the question, "Why do you need more land when you aren't even using what you have?" Similar questions include, "When are you going to build the park?" or "What good is all that land just lying there and not being used?"

We have to explain that land is being used when people are looking at it or enjoying it in a great variety of ways. A television set is something we only look at and listen to—it doesn't do the dishes, sweep the floor, cook our meals, or wash our clothes. Yet most people say they use their television sets.

Natural areas already have been "built" by nature. All a natural-type park system does is make it possible for people to enjoy and appreciate the land for what it is. And we have to remind people how the land is being used twenty-four hours a day by thousands of plants and animals. Some of these, such as the insects which pollinate our fruits, travel great distances from their homes in the parklands. Natural areas near our cities also help to improve the quality of the air we breathe. So, in a sense, we are using such natural areas even when we are miles away from them.

WHY SOME PEOPLE RESENT NATURE

When I'm with a group of children in a spring woods I can't say, "Look at all the pretty wildflowers; I really did a good job in making them bloom today."

No one can take credit for the natural development of the Grand Canyon or other outstanding features of our land. This doesn't bother those of us who are willing to accept nature for what it is; we still feel that we're a part of our natural surroundings. This is not true for all people, however.

Many cannot feel that they're part of something unless they can manage, manipulate, or control it. They'll feel a part of a natural area only if they can plant trees, change the landscape, create artificial lakes, construct buildings in the woods, or leave some other mark upon the land. It seems a shame but that's the way it is. Some even resent nature because they cannot take credit for the wonders and beauty created by nature.

LESSON OF THE DODDER

Dodder is a plant that grows as a vine; it has no chlorophyll, has no leaves, and is a parasite. The plants do produce flowers and seeds.

Upon sprouting, the seedling grows up out of the ground, twines around its host plant, and inserts suckers through which it obtains water and nutrients. As it grows, it breaks away from its roots and loses all contact with the soil. As its host plant weakens and dies, the dodder is left helpless and also dies.

The human race, in many instances, has lost all contact with the earth and is somewhat parasitic upon technology and the efforts of a few. If technology and our artificial means of survival ever wear out or let us down, we'll find ourselves in the same predicament as the dodder. Most people have lost the ability to live off the land.

A MESSAGE TO OTHERS

In this chapter concerning various things to say and do we have provided a combined total of more than 300 different interpretive techniques, concepts of interpretation, and examples of interpretive information. Few have had anything to do with identification of a particular species. Would your not knowing the difference between a red oak and a black oak take anything away from what has been discussed and suggested?

When you're with other adults, be sure to drive this point home whenever the opportunity presents itself. Be sure, too, to remind children how much fun they have had and can continue to have without having to make something complicated out of nature.

I hope you understand why I feel rather disgusted when someone approaches me and says, "Sure, you can lead kids on nature walks because you know the names of everything, but what about a dummy like me who can't tell the difference between an oak and an elm?"